POINTS OF ORDER

by

GLADYS WALKER, J.P.

◆　　◆

FOURTH EDITION

◆　　◆

LONDON:
SHAW & SONS LTD.,
Shaway House,
Lower Sydenham,
SE26 5AE

First published .... September 1969

Second Edition .... May 1971

Third Edition .... September 1976

Fourth Edition .... November 1987

ISBN 0 7219 0402 5

CONTENTS

CONTENTS

CONTENTS

INTRODUCTION TO FOURTH EDITION

In the introduction to the first edition of this book in July 1969 I wrote that our complex society is made up of many and varied groups, organisations, institutions and councils, all of them seeking to serve the community in their own particular sphere of activity. In turn, these bodies are served by a vast number of admirable people who give of their time and energies, almost always in a voluntary capacity, to serve as officers, committee members and the like. Indeed, no country in the world has a wider network of voluntary service than our own.

One item on the agenda at most annual general meetings is that of appointment of officers and sometimes when it becomes necessary to replace a long serving officer, an organisation has difficulty in finding a successor. All too often we hear the plea, "But I've never done anything like that before". This book has been written in the hope that it will be of some assistance to the many people already taking part in community life, from the civic leader of a large authority officiating at important functions to the honorary secretary of the village social club arranging less formal gatherings, and in particular, to those who "have never done anything like that before", as they make their début into community affairs.

The second edition in November 1970 gave me the opportunity of revising, correcting and up-dating the original work and the third edition in August 1976 took account of new laws dealing with local government reforms and women's rights. I also extended that edition to include a new section on public speaking.

Now a decade later, I have completely re-arranged and up-dated this fourth edition to bring it into line with our more informal social order.

I would like to express my sincere thanks to kind correspondents who took the trouble to send me their comments in the past. I hope that interested readers will let me know about any errors or omissions in this edition.

I wish to record my grateful thanks to The Registrar of The Lord Chamberlains' Office for so patiently dealing with my several queries; to Brian M. Malley of Calderdale Magistrates' Clerk's Office for the trouble he took to supply me with the latest criminal statistics; to my sister Edna Mitsy Howarth for her help with the text; to Dr. Giles Havergal, O.B.E. for his candid criticism and helpful suggestions and somewhat belatedly to Donald Sartain who, way back in 1969 when I was undecided about a title for this work, suggested "Points of Order".

G.W.

Heptonstall,
West Yorkshire

Chapter I
TAKING PART IN PUBLIC LIFE

1. GETTING INVOLVED

The burgeoning of new movements covering every feature of our modern society seems to be never ending. Many of these groups start out with a mere handful of like-minded enthusiasts; some are intended for short-term once-only projects, whereas others go on to become national organisations with nationwide branches.

It has been known for more than one person to become so involved with their particular cause that they aspire to serve their community in a wider sphere of public service, as for instance the "Save our village school" group member who seeks election to the local council in the hope of being able to influence the way the schools are run.

Just as long established organisations work to rules of conduct and observe generally accepted procedures so any new group will have to draw up a set of rules to help them achieve their desired aims.

In spite of today's more relaxed attitudes to tradition it has been proved through all the years of social change and fashion that there are certain customs which if observed make for an ordered society and there are common courtesies which if kept, make life pleasanter for all. The following chapters deal with many of these customs and practices so far as our community life is concerned.

2. ON BEING ELECTED TO LEAD

All organisations, societies, groups or councils elect one of their number to guide them in their deliberations and to represent them in their community at large. The majority of those who hold office by election, be it as chairman of the village social club, president of the chamber of trade and commerce, or mayor, even lord mayor of his or her native town or adopted borough, almost always carry out their duties extremely well and having earned their preferment by long and loyal service, when they are elected to lead, they toil even harder in the interests of their society or town, so winning the admiration and respect of a much wider circle of people.

3. THOSE CALLED UPON TO SHARE THE LIMELIGHT

In spite of the various women's liberation movements and the work of the Equal Opportunities Commission it is sad to relate that there are still far more men than women taking part in public life and it often happens that when a man assumes office for the first time, his wife, who will be sharing the limelight with him, has little or no experience of public life and in many cases is extremely nervous. After a time, however, this nervousness can be replaced by the ability to carry out public functions with grace and charm and it has been known for an extremely nervous person to take her own place in public life after a period acting as hostess for her husband.

Nevertheless, the nervous housewife who is accustomed to little more than the committee procedure of the Mothers' Union or the Townswomen's Guild can find it something of an ordeal when her husband is elected as mayor or even lord mayor and she is called upon to act as hostess to a Royal visitor at some important function in the new Civic Centre. Not only is she called upon to support her husband in all he does, but she is expected to plunge herself with enthusiasm into opening fêtes, bazaars, presenting prizes at school sports and thanking the local Soroptimists for having her at their annual dinner—and none of this of her own seeking.

With our close friends we can relax completely and be ourselves, for they understand us for what we are and in spite of our shortcomings continue to be our friends, but with people we are meeting for the first time or with people we know only slightly, there is need for a little more restraint. For the housewife who is leaving behind her household chores to appear in full evening dress as first lady of the municipality at the Rotary Club Ladies' Festival or some other local function which ranks as a highlight in the "social round", there are a few golden rules to be borne in mind.

The first thing to remember is that without doubt the eyes of all will be taking in every detail of dress, speech and general behaviour, in fact no single facet of grooming or conduct will be unnoticed and if any detail falls short of the accepted standard, then you can rest assured it will be remarked upon in the community!

There will be those who are comparing the lady with her predecessor and those who feel it is their duty to shower encouragement and their own particular brand of praise on the newcomer, whether or not it has been asked for, or is merited. We have all met them—the small town social climbers who must "be in" and are almost always shallow and insincere. It is inevitable that, when face to face with this type of person, one has to listen to their gushing chatter, but one must beware of it, for it is very harmful and in some cases can be cruel.

Year after year I listened to this type of social climber going on in their sycophantic way with such remarks as, "Oh, I think you are the best Mayor we have ever had". The harm is irreparable when they are believed!

Even allowing for the fact that we all have our own ideas as to what passes for small talk and polite behaviour, that kind of tongue-in-the-cheek social nicety is really unhelpful.

4. THE ROLE OF WOMEN IN THE COMMUNITY

With the passing of the Sex Discrimination Act and the Equal Pay Act, women achieved what is probably the biggest step forward in their hard fought campaign for equality since they were given the vote by the Reform Act of 1918.

The Sex Discrimination Act makes it unlawful to discriminate against either sex in the fields of education, training and employment and in the supply of goods, facilities and services, but it is not possible to legislate against social attitudes and outlooks and time alone will reveal whether or not the Act brings about the hoped-for results. Safe to say that no mortgage company or building society can refuse a woman a mortgage on equal terms with her male counterpart nowadays.

The appointment of our present Prime Minister, Margaret Thatcher, as the first woman to lead a major political party was one of several "firsts" for women in the year before the Sex Discrimination Act became law. Dame Rose Heilbron, Q.C., who had the distinction of being appointed the first woman Recorder in this country in 1956, in turn became the first woman to take her place as a judge at the Old Bailey.

The appointment of Lavinia, Duchess of Norfolk as Lord Lieutenant of West Sussex on the death of her husband who had held the position previously, made her the first woman to hold such office in England and Wales and that was followed by Baroness Phillips serving for a time as Her Majesty's Lord Lieutenant of Greater London.

In the field of business, multiple retail trade and commerce we have grown accustomed to hearing about enterprising young men who rock the City's financial institutions from time to time, yet the names of Margery Hurst of the Brook Street Bureau, Mary

15

Quant and the late Laura Ashley stand out as women who have made it to the top in big business in our country.

In 1919, the American born Nancy, Lady Astor, was elected Unionist Member of Parliament for a division of Plymouth, being the first woman elected to sit in the House of Commons. She held the seat in subsequent elections for some years and won a distinct place for herself in the House and in our history books, yet almost seventy years on, in national government and at local level, we have only a small percentage of women as Members of Parliament and council members.

Bearing in mind that national and local government control most aspects of our affairs, women need to work much harder to make their voices heard.

5. APPOINTMENT AS A JUSTICE OF THE PEACE

The English system of lay magistracy is more than six hundred years old, having survived the reigns of thirty-one monarchs and the period of the commonwealth, and although there have been changes in the status, duties and functions of the Justices, the system is unique and one which is the envy of many other nations.

There has been a mistaken impression in the minds of many people that Justices of the Peace are appointed as a reward for past services to the community or to a particular political party, although publicity given to the need for enlarging the field of choice and facilitating selection from all sections of the community may do something to dispel this widespread misunderstanding.

Justices of the Peace are appointed on behalf of the Sovereign by the Lord Chancellor, except in the County of Lancashire where the Sovereign is also Duke of Lancaster and where appointments are made by the Chancellor of the Duchy of Lancaster.

The Central Office of Information, on behalf of the Lord Chancellor and the Chancellor of the Duchy of Lancaster, has issued a pamphlet pointing out that Justices are appointed to the Commissions of the Peace based on recommendations of local advisory committees, the members of which are drawn from all sections of the community, but whose names are never published.

The first and much the most important consideration is that those nominated should be personally suitable in point of character, integrity and understanding for the work they will have to perform. The pamphlet stresses that in no circumstances will the Lord Chancellor appoint any one as a reward for past services of any kind, nor will the Lord Chancellor or the Chancellor of the Duchy of Lancaster appoint a person who is a whole time paid political agent.

From time to time, as the need to recruit new magistrates arises, advertisements are inserted in local newspapers inviting members of the public who are interested in serving as justices to apply to their local Magistrates' Clerk. Anyone can recommend candidates for appointment as Justices of the Peace and again this should be done by writing to your local Magistrates' Clerk, marking the letter "Private and Confidential".

Because of the continuing increase in the complexity and scope of magistrates' duties in Court, newly appointed magistrates are required to undergo a training course, partly before they begin to adjudicate and partly during the first year of appointment.

Recent criminal statistics reveal that in one year some 2,184,000 cases were dealt with in the magistrates' courts of this country by comparison with only 90,500 cases tried by the higher courts. This means that lay magistrates deal, on average, with over 90% of all persons charged with criminal offences. Nearly two hundred and fifty thousand magistrates' courts are held throughout the country in the course of each year, which means that on average there are something like a thousand courts sitting every working day, including Saturdays, and it has been known for Sir Thomas Skyrme, former Secretary of Commissions to the Lord Chancellor and Chairman of the Magistrates' Association's Council and Executive Committee, himself an active Justice, to be called out to take a special court in the City of London on Boxing Day.

In addition to sitting in court, there is the work which falls to magistrates under the Licensing Acts, Adoption of Children and Young Persons Acts, taking of declarations and keeping up to date with the new legislation which affects the administration of justice in the magistrates' courts, from which it will be obvious that by far the vast majority of justice administered in this country is administered by ordinary men and women fully representative of the law abiding public and the British taxpayer owes much to those who undertake this work.

Due to our system of lay magistracy, we have, in relation to population, a far smaller number of whole-time professional judges than any other western democracy and the cost of administering justice here is by far the smallest percentage of the national budget.

It therefore follows that the impression most people gain of English justice by first hand knowledge arises more from the acts of magistrates than from any other source and for this reason it is imperative that at all times the demeanour of justices should be beyond reproach, both in and out of court.

Some years ago there was a section of the magistracy known to favour the idea of wearing some form of robe in Court but there were those who were against this on the grounds that the magistrates are "of the people". Whatever the arguments for or against the question of attire, there can be no doubt that the most suitable dress for a male magistrate is a dark day suit, leaving off masonic, rotary and trade union emblems and the like. A woman magistrate is most suitably dressed in a quiet outfit without an ostentatious display of jewels. In this way will it appear more obvious to defendants and witnesses that justice is being administered without bias and without fear or favour, affection or ill will.

When signing documents or one's signature at any time, it is not correct for a Justice of the Peace to add the letters "J.P." after the signature. The Lord Chancellor has expressed the opinion that the suffix ought not to be used on professional or business notepaper, on the ground that this might lead to the supposition that the office of magistrate is being used for the furthering of professional or business interests, but he sees no serious objection to the use of the letters being placed after the names of directors of public companies on documents such as company prospectuses. Similarly the Lord Chancellor considers it to be undesirable for the suffix to be used on matter relating to candidature for parliamentary or local elections. Full details for the order of precedence and for the placing of this suffix will be found in Chapter V.

Although many of the cases dealt with by magistrates may seem trifling and sometimes amusing to the Bench, it should be remembered that the defendants may feel very deeply about the charges and for this reason flippancy of any kind on the part of the justices is much to be deplored.

When present on the Bench, justices should never allow their attention to become distracted from the business before the court. *Sub rosa* comments causing smirks and titters among members of the bench can create a misleading and disturbing impression, so much so that on one occasion an offender, after being sentenced complained . . . "But the old b . . . s never listened!".

6. WHAT DO I WEAR?

(a) Women's Outfits

Television newscoverage of The Queen's two daughters-in-law in their many stunning outfits is a constant reminder that Great Britain's billion pound fashion industry, better known to young people as the rag trade, is bigger than the whole of our car industry and twice as big as the aerospace industry and is greatly influenced by our trend setting Princess of Wales and her Sloane-set sister-in-law, the Duchess of York.

Just as their Royal Highnesses have created their own royal image, so anyone in the public eye needs to seek a fashion image befitting her age and figure, not forgetting her bank balance, as well as the demands likely to be made on her wardrobe.

With all outfits it is important to pay attention to accessories, for all too often the wrong handbag or gloves can be a let down to an otherwise well chosen outfit.

(b) Shoes

In order to be fully at ease it is essential that one's outfit and especially one's shoes, are completely comfortable. When invited to tour a new industrial complex it will not be possible to relax and be interested in the tour if one's toes are pinched in narrow fitting shoes with heels so high one feels one is walking on stilts. On so many occasions we see The Princess of Wales wearing attractive low heeled court shoes in colours to match her outfits.

(c) Hats

The sixties and seventies saw the almost total decline of the millinery trade, as hairdressing salons created first the bouffant, then the beehive followed by the straight shoulder length hair style, making the wearing of conventional hats a rather tricky business.

Since her marriage to the Prince of Wales our millinery designers and manufacturers have had reason to be grateful to The Princess of Wales for the boost she has given to their share of the fashion industry by the many jaunty and eye-catching hats she wears. Look-alikes of these hats are very popular, especially with younger women and some of them are very becoming to the more mature women.

Her Royal Highness the Princess Royal manages to cope with her long hair in a clever way by adopting a different hair style for each of the trendy hats she wears but this is not a practical proposition for many women, especially if they have day-time and evening engagements with little time between for changing and dressing their hair, let alone visiting a hairdresser.

The Prime Minister is seen immaculately groomed but hatless as she makes day-time visits but on more formal occasions, such as the Opening of Parliament and Remembrance Sunday she is seen wearing a hat which matches her coat.

When attending a gathering where it is expected that guests will be seated in rows, women should show consideration by wearing smaller hats in order that people sitting behind can see without having to crane their necks.

When attending a function starting after 6 p.m. women can discard hats even if wearing day dress.

The woman who is invited to present prizes at the local school sports on a windy day should resist the temptation to wear that large brimmed hat which perches on top of her head and has to be supported by a hand against every puff of wind that comes along. It will be possible for her to be comfortable and really enjoy the sports if she wears a pull-on hat firmly in place on her head and shoes with low or medium height heels suitable for walking on grass.

For the woman who is not a patroness of haute couture and does not seek to win the title of local trend setter, it is a good idea to wear well fitting clothes and hats of the particular style in which she feels most comfortable and our Royal Ladies have set many examples of this.

The Queen Mother has made the loose fitting edge to edge coat with bracelet length sleeves her own favourite style as she goes about tirelessly carrying out her many public engagements.

Many older people remember the late Queen Mary, grandmother of our present Queen, who favoured hats styled in the shape of toques. Early in life Queen Mary found that the toque suited her and she enjoyed wearing it and no matter how fashions changed Queen Mary continued to wear her famous toques to the end of her long life.

(d) Men's Day Dress

Morning dress is seldom worn now, excepting in Court circles, the City of London with its Lord Mayor, Sheriffs and Aldermen and perhaps by the civic heads of one or two other large cities and then only on strictly formal occasions, such as visits by senior members of the Royal Family or a Head of a foreign state or for attending a national religious service. In fact the invitations to The Royal Wedding of 1986, between His Royal Highness The Prince Andrew and Sarah Ferguson stated Morning Dress or Lounge suits.

When attending gatherings in a representative capacity a smart dark lounge suit has the advantage of providing the best background for any badge of office or medals which may be worn.

(e) Men's Hats

Gentlemen wearing hats should remove them when entering a building, when the National Anthem is played and when returning a salute to Colours or paying tribute at a cenotaph.

(f) Evening Dress

At all times it is important to make sure that the dress stated on an invitation is strictly adhered to.

Although more and more invitations now state "Black tie" or "Dinner Jacket" or even "Dress optional" and there are fewer of the strictly formal occasions where an invitation states "Evening dress and decorations", where this is indicated, it is a clear indication from the host that he expects his gentlemen guests to wear white tie and tail coat and ladies to wear full evening dress with gloves. If appropriate clothes are not owned and it is not feasible to buy or hire them, then serious consideration should be given to the advisability of declining the invitation. Few of us would have the temerity to disregard the wishes of our host on such a matter.

7. WHEN DO I APPLAUD?

Although most of us have at some time or other attended an official gathering as one of the crowd, it can be quite another thing to attend as a principal guest. For the wife whose husband is called upon to speak on the toast list, there is the question as to when she joins in the applause. Where a principal guest is toasted and called upon to respond, the proposer of the toast will without doubt, make reference to the presence of the wife supporting her husband, in which event the wife would not join in the applause at the end of the toast in which she has received a mention. Her husband in responding, would thank the proposer for his remarks and the other guests for the way in which they have received the toast and would naturally offer thanks on behalf

25

of his wife. Again there would be no need for the wife to join in the applause.

At other gatherings or meetings when a vote of thanks is moved to the principal guest, the wife need not join in the applause.

8. SITTING ON A PLATFORM

A lady's skirt which is around knee length when standing can pose quite a problem for its wearer when sitting on a platform in full view of the local populace. Although pantie hose are a great boon in this connection, it is important to learn how to sit on a platform—with ankles and knees held firmly together, please ladies!

How many times have we seen the unthinking heavily-built lady take her place on a public platform and sit in a most ungainly and unladylike way? Please, ladies, do give some time to making yourselves aware of the importance of HOW TO SIT and HOW NOT TO SIT on a platform.

9. BEING PHOTOGRAPHED

An inevitable consequence of taking part in public affairs is to be pictured in the local press occasionally. Those who have a weight problem should remember that dark coloured garments are kinder to their outline and especially so in photographs.

10. MAKING-UP IN PUBLIC

Every woman knows that it is "not done" to make a show of applying make-up in public, but if attending a gathering where one is to speak following a meal, it can be quite off-putting to have to get up and speak knowing that one's lips are pale, having lost all their lipstick during the meal. There is no doubt about it, most women find make-up something of a morale booster and on such occasions it cannot be incorrect to follow the example of Her Majesty the Queen and Princess Margaret, who discreetly take out a mirror and handkerchief and re-apply their lipstick once the meal is over. Princess Margaret has been seen to use a red handkerchief for this operation. But that is the extent of making-up in public and it must be done quickly and discreetly. Combing one's hair or bringing out a powder puff is inadvisable.

11. SIGNATURES AND SIGNING THE VISITORS' BOOK

How many of us on receiving a letter signed "A. Blank" have had to go to no end of trouble when replying to find out if the writer is male or female? How much easier it would be if all women would remember to sign their full Christian name,—"Ann Blank". If a married woman and not known to her correspondent, it would be helpful to add underneath the signature in capitals—Mrs. JOHN BLANK, or add Mrs. in brackets after the signature as follows—Ann Blank (Mrs.) but never should a woman

27

sign "Mrs. Ann Blank". The marital status is not part of the signature.

When asked to sign a visitor's book, a woman should sign her usual signature, that is, "Ann Blank" and if she is visiting as Mayoress of her Borough or President of the Townswomen's Guild, it would be appropriate for her to add after her signature— "Mayoress of B ....", or "President of B...................... Townswomens .... Guild", as the case may be.

Letters such as J.P., or decorations such as M.B.E. are not part of the signature and should not be added to it. If the writer wishes to indicate these they should be printed at the top of the writer's personal notepaper in the following way—

From: Councillor Arthur B. See, M.B.E., J.P.,

An alternative way of indicating them is to have the full name typed underneath the signature, as below—

Usual signature — Arthur B. See

Block letters   (Councillor Arthur B. See,
                       M.B.E., J.P.,).

Both these approaches overcome problems for the person who has to address a letter to a correspondent who has cultivated one of those illegible signatures we see so often these days.

12. TESTIMONIALS, REFERENCES, FOREWORDS ETC.

Responsible members of the community are frequently asked to supply testimonials or act as referees for persons needing evidence of their ability or character and sometimes their financial status.

Persons requiring testimonials or referees to vouch for their integrity should always make a point of asking, either verbally or in writing, the permission of the person they propose to name as a referee. It is the height of impudence to assume that because you have a nodding acquaintance with the vicar or a local dignitary, he or she will be willing, or for that matter, able, to testify to your ability and integrity in the glowing terms called for to secure you that new appointment or extra bank loan. On the contrary, it could be the the only characteristic of yours that the vicar or local dignitary can bring to mind, is one that puts you at a distinct disadvantage. Think carefully before naming referees, select people who know you well and be sure to ask their permission before offering their names.

Those asked for information concerning another's character and ability should be at pains to give only accurate information. Many government departments, business firms and finance houses issue printed forms asking a variety of questions. When not absolutely certain about the answer to any particular question, it is far better to state that you do not feel able to answer such a question, rather than attempt to give an answer that could be misleading.

Forewords, etc.

A popular source of revenue for events organised in aid of charity is the souvenir programme, with the local president or civic head being invited to contribute a foreword commending the good cause which is to benefit from the event. Notable among these are the university rag magazines.

Those asked to supply the foreword are almost always unaware of the remainder of the material which is to be included in the programme and for this reason should exercise caution in agreeing to sponsor the publication. It has been the unhappy lot of a number of civic leaders in recent times, to give much thought to the preparation of a message containing well chosen words commending the good cause which is to benefit from the sale of the publication, and to allow their photograph in which they appear wearing full mayoral insignia, to appear alongside the message, only to find that the remainder of the magazine contains sick minded matter bordering on pornography.

Before agreeing to support any publication, it is advisable to insist on seeing a complete draft or proof of the entire publication. Only in this way can much embarrassment be avoided, for indignant townspeople are inclined to have a poor opinion of the judgement of a civic head who makes the feeble excuse that "I was unaware of the contents of the magazine."

13. HUMOUR

Anyone in the public eye needs to cultivate and at all times maintain a sense of humour, coupled with the ability to laugh at him or herself.

Over the years the Royal Family have on many occasions revealed this trait and shewn us how to make the best of a bad situation, even going so far as to quip when things go wrong.

The most recent example was during the Royal Tour of New Zealand by The Queen and Prince Philip in February 1986, when in a deplorable incident in Auckland two misguided young women threw eggs at the Royal Land Rover, one of which spattered the right hand side of the Queen's coat. We can only guess at the momentary shock this must have caused to The Queen and Prince Philip but newsreel pictures of the occasion shewed their calm unruffled reaction.

How relieved the New Zealand Prime Minister and his people must have been when, speaking at a banquet in Wellington only a few hours later, The Queen commented that, "New Zealand has long been renowned for its dairy produce", adding good humouredly, "but I prefer my New Zealand egg for breakfast".

Chapter II

ENTERTAINING AND BEING ENTERTAINED

1. RECEIVING GUESTS

A host and hostess should always shake hands, when greeting and saying goodbye to their guests, be it a formal reception or an informal social evening. Ladies wearing gloves need not remove them when shaking hands. A man should always remove his right glove when shaking hands.

2. INTRODUCTIONS

We are all accustomed to today's informal introductions—"Jane Bee—Jon Tee", "Samantha this is Gemma". These may be acceptable in some circles but give no indication of who is being introduced to whom.

A host and hostess entertaining on behalf of their community or organisation often find it necessary to carry out introductions and these should be done bearing in mind a few simple rules of convention, such as—

    (*a*) A man is introduced to a woman and when this is done the man's name is spoken last, for example, "Mrs. Hay, may I present to you Mr. Jon Tee, our Club Secretary".

        If introducing an elderly man to a younger person, then the above rule can be reversed in deference to age. In just the same way, if introducing a distinguished visitor to a local person then the visitor is named first, irrespective of age or sex, as follows, "Mr. Mayor, may I introduce Mrs. Gee who is a member of our Society".

(b) It is usual for a single woman to be introduced to a married woman, e.g. "Mrs. Kay, I would like to introduce Miss Tee", but if the married woman is very much younger then it would be appropriate to reverse the order and introduce the married woman to the older single woman. "Miss Old, I don't think you have met Mrs. Young who is our newest member".

(c) Younger people are always introduced to older people,—"Mrs Ward, this is Stephen Taylor".

To sum up, the principle is to present the man to the woman; less important people to the more distinguished people and youngsters to older people. You can reverse the rule of introducing a man to a woman when the man is much older than the woman, just as the rule of introducing a single woman to a married woman is reversed when the married woman is much younger than the single person. Men in the same age group have no special priority excepting where one holds a high public office.

When introducing a woman to a stranger it is helpful to state her marital status, *i.e.* Mrs. or Miss, unless you know that she belongs to that breed of trendy theorists who claim to be Ms., in which case the christian and surname will have to suffice.

On all occasions it is usual to reply to an introduction with, "How do you do".

It is in order for a woman to remain seated when introduced to anyone unless the person is another woman much older than herself or is a very distinguished person but men should always rise when being introduced to a person of either sex who is standing.

When attending a formal function preceded by a reception where guests are announced by a Master of Ceremonies, the man should give the names to whoever is making the announcement and as they are announced the couple should move forward to be greeted by their host and hostess, the woman being the first to shake hands.

When called upon to receive and make presentations to members of the Royal Family a careful study of the details outlined in paragraphs 2 and 4 of Chapter VI (pages 106 and 114 *post*) will be found helpful.

3. WHEN TO LEAVE

It will be readily understood that if attending a Royal event, a guest should never leave before the Royal Guest.

Although it is customary still for many invitations to indicate the time for "cars" or "transport",—in other words the time a function will end and guests are expected to leave, there are occasions when the time for leaving is not stated, as in the case of less formal parties. On these occasions it is important for guests to show some consideration for their host and hostess and avoid overstaying their welcome, particular when attending in an official capacity, representing their community or organisation.

When invited for luncheon, guests should leave not later than 3.30 p.m. unless invited to stay on for some specific purpose, an example of which would be where guests lunched with the Directors of an industrial concern and were invited to tour the works to see the production plant immediately after luncheon.

Afternoon tea guests should leave not later than 5 p.m. whereas if high tea is served at say 5.30 p.m. or 6 p.m. then guests should make a point of leaving not later than 7.30 p.m. When invited for cocktails at 6 p.m. considerate guests will have left by 8 p.m. and it is absolutely unforgivable to be "hanging-on" at 8.30 p.m. On the other hand, if guests are invited for cocktails at 8 p.m. then they should leave between 10 p.m. and 10.30 p.m.

After a dinner party where the time of departure is not stated, representative guests should leave by 11 p.m. and in no event later than 11.30 p.m.

The Royal Navy, who are without doubt expert hosts, often hold cocktail parties for local dignitaries when paying goodwill visits in ports. Almost always these parties commence at 6 p.m. the aim being that all guests will have departed by 8.30 p.m. and dinner can then be served in the wardroom at 9 p.m. On such occasions, a local dignitary who is on board when 9 p.m. arrives has blotted his copy book in no uncertain manner and is a source of much embarrassment to his host.

There is a delightful story told of Dr. Vaughan, Head Master of Harrow, in the middle of the last century, who acquired a reputation for getting rid of unwanted guests. His technique was to enquire from the shyest guest present in a loud voice, "Must you go? Can't you stay?" History relates that within seconds of this remark being made, the entire company of hangers-on would disappear.

North-country people are famed for their bluntness and plain speaking, but not all would be able to follow the example of a certain Yorkshire host, who, when coming upon a guest who was out-staying his welcome, remarked, "Oh, there you are. Haven't you gone yet?".

4. ATTENDING A UNIVERSITY DEGREE CONFERMENT

A University Degree Conferment can be a very interesting and colourful event, particularly if there are Honorary Graduands taking part. Academicians and Mayors are invited to take part in the Chancellor's Procession wearing their robes.

Parents of graduands are allocated reserved seats for the ceremony and should be present in good time for the commencement. It is appropriate for women to wear hats on these occasions.

5. SCHOOL SPEECH DAYS OR PRIZE-GIVING

These can be pleasant occasions, especially so for the parents of bright pupils receiving awards.

Parents, and mothers in particular, will do well to remember that a sensitive son or daughter will give a far warmer welcome if you are wearing a reasonably sober outfit and not that outrageous hat that causes everyone to titter.

6. REPLYING TO INVITATIONS

One of the most vexing tasks confronting the organisers of a function which is by invitation, is that of getting in the replies. In recent years there appears to have grown up within the British race, an innate dislike to R.S.V.P.ing! From experience it has been found that even sending a stamped addressed reply card does not bring in 100 per cent. replies, thus posing the problem as to what happens to the stamps on the cards. Do the recipients steam them off and use them for some other purpose? Be that as it may, the fact remains that the organisers of such functions are deserving of the utmost sympathy, for they are expected to know as if by instinct whether or not certain people will be presenting themselves at a function. Such remarks as, "But you know I ALWAYS come", are just not good enough, especially when the organiser has a very clear recollection of the fact that you were on holiday at the time of the previous gathering!

Chapter III
STAND UP, SPEAK UP AND . . .

1. SPEECH AND SPEAKING WELL

The late Lord Birkett of Ulverston, who was a great lover of the spoken word, once said, "Wherever people go they are judged by the way they speak", and few of us would argue with that. Just as music can give pleasure to the ears, so can a well modulated, pleasant speaking voice.

I think it is true to say that quite a high proportion of our population are influenced in their speech by what they hear on radio and television and as stations and programmes have grown in numbers and hours of broadcasting have increased, with more and more people taking part, the result has been a steady decline in the quality of speech.

Some of the present newscasters, including a few of the women, speak well and are easy to follow but some of the chat-show hosts and presenters of children's programmes are guilty of slaughtering the English language.

The amateur speaker would do well to spend some time listening to the announcers who broadcast the English transmissions of the BBC World Service programme which is available in the United Kingdom on wavelengths 648 or 463. They speak standard English, know how to pronounce words and their pronouncements make listening a pleasure.

2. REGIONAL ACCENTS

Regional customs make us a more interesting people and regional accents, conveying the warmth of the natural voice, backed by a sound knowledge of the English language express the personality of the speaker and can be attractive to listen to and are infinitely preferable to an assumed "Oxford accent" or what, during my younger days, northerners sometimes referred to as "semi-detached posh talk".

I spent sixteen years of my career working and living in the London area before returning to my native Pennine area for my retirement. I went south with my northern accent; I think it is true to say I retained it throughout those sixteen years and it is still intact today. During the time I was in the south, on more than one occasion I was introduced to people and the concluding remark to the introduction would be, "and she comes from the north", in tones which implied that the north is some far distant outback! Lord James of Rusholme, the former Vice-Chancellor of York University has gone on record as saying, "most southerners feel they should be inoculated before going north".

With the decline of industry in the north more and more people from the provinces and all parts of the country have converged on the home counties and regional accents tend to have been replaced by what some people regard as the more genteel, softer-vowel tones of the south, but conversation will become very dull if it is to be carried on in what has been described as, "the glib colour supplement manner of southern England".

Whatever our accents few of us would wish to take part in public life with an accent like Eliza Doolittle but Professor Higgins needs to come early into our lives and to work long and hard if we are to achieve Eliza's success. We have all suffered from and with the person of mature years, who after a few hurried elocution lessons, stands on a platform and makes his or her speech in tense clipped tones, with little or no feeling coming over to the audience. It is far better to be oneself and speak naturally, for only in this way will the warmth and real depth of personality come across. Shakespeare wrote of Cordelia in "King Lear", her voice was ever soft, gentle and low, an excellent thing in woman", but Shakespeare did not have to contend with all the background noises of twentieth century living and it can be most irritating to try to converse with a person who mumbles, even if from shyness. On the other hand, people with loud voices carrying on general conversation in a confined area should remember that everyone present does not wish to be forced to listen to their conversation, no matter how scintillating it may be! Don't forget that a discreet silence can earn you the reputation of being a good listener.

3. "U" AND "NON-U" WORDS

There is a lot of snobbery attached to the question of "U" and "non-U" and "In" and "Out" words and much of it amounts to little short of arrogant non-sense and silly affectation. It is not to our credit to try to change our natural choice of words just to please the language snobs.

4. SPEAKING BEFORE AN AUDIENCE

More than three hundred and fifty years ago Francis Bacon wrote, "Reading maketh a full man; conference a ready man; and writing an exact man." From reading we glean ideas clothed in words to help us to live "full" lives. By conference, i.e., conversation, discussion or debate, we learn how to be "ready" to express ourselves and the expression of our ideas is facilitated and clarified if we first of all write them down and, if necessary, re-write them until we have them in "exact" form.

The newcomer to public life is almost always inexperienced in speaking before an audience and sensitive people do find this somewhat nerve-shattering at first. With practice it is possible to gain confidence and acquire an easy technique but only if careful thought and preparation are given to what is being said and the way in which it is delivered.

Generally, audiences re-act favourably to a little diffidence but most people are less nervous if facing an audience fully prepared.

Those who are invited to make a speech should regard the invitation as an honour, bearing in mind that the average audience is prepared to give a speaker their time and attention and time is a valuable commodity these days. In return for this, the least a speaker can do is to devote a good deal of time and thought to preparing the speech.

To paraphrase our English poet and dramatist, Ben Jonson, "Any fool may talk, but only a wise man, thoroughly prepared, can make a good speech".

Sir Winston Churchill is known once to have advised a new Member of Parliament, eager to make his maiden speech on his first day in the House, "Better to have people wondering why you don't speak than wondering why you do".

5. PREPARATION

The Roman orator and philosopher Cicero, many of whose letters and speeches survive, taught that there were five essential rules for public speaking, these being—

(i) Decide on the exact subject of your speech then read all you can about it; afterwards think deeply through the whole subject.

(ii) Prepare a draft in three parts, (a) Introduction, (b) Main body of speech, and (c) Summary and conclusion.

(iii) Clothe the speech with well chosen words and carefully phrased sentences.

(iv) Memorise the speech and rehearse it over and over again.

(v) Finally when you arrive before your audience, deliver the speech with dignity and grace.

These five rules are just as applicable today as at the time of the Roman Empire but our twentieth century life-style has made it essential to add a sixth rule—brevity.

To enlarge on Cicero's rules—

(*i*) Make a point of studying other speakers, both on television and in person. Watch them closely as well as listening to their method of delivery, and, if possible pay special attention to the feeling prevailing amongst the audience as a speaker moves from point to point in the course of the speech.

Be sure to visit the local reference library and seek the help of the librarian. You will be surprised at the number of works published on your particular subject, in addition to those you already know about. Study as many as you can so as to develop your knowledge of the subject over as broad a spectrum as possible and to deepen your interest in it. You cannot explain to an audience what you do not understand yourself nor can you create enthusiasm in others for a subject in which you are only mildly interested.

(*ii*) Jot down all your ideas as they occur to you. Keep a pad and pencil by your bed; you are sure to wake up thinking of something and if you don't make a note of it there and then it could be gone for ever.

The next step is to form a structure for your speech by arranging all your material so that it tells a cogent and coherent story. The introduction should clearly state the subject about which you are going to speak followed by a brief history of it. The main body of the speech should be divided into several parts, each dealing with a specific idea. Round off by summarising your ideas and stressing the salient points you wish to leave with your audience.

For obvious reasons the introduction and conclusion are the most important parts of any speech. In the introduction you must arouse the interest of your audience. Having done this you carry them with you through the main body of your speech and in your short, but well rounded off summary, you hope to leave your audience wishing you had gone on longer. A much happier situation than having them breathe sighs of relief that at long last you have shut up.

(*iii*) When your skeleton speech is prepared you should go on to clothe it with well chosen words and carefully phrased sentences, and the best source of help for this is as wide a range of reading as possible—books, magazines and newspapers on all topics. Read **all** the newspapers you can, not only the quality and the popular editions, but the sensational ones as well from time to time. If you come across a new word, look it up in the dictionary if it is an orthodox one, or enquire of your younger more "with-it" acquaintances if it is a trendy one.

The judge peering over his glasses, asking counsel for a definition of a current expression or word is a familiar and facile source of humour in most television dramas. In real life such remoteness from contemporary language and usage is isolating and inhibiting.

Apt quotations can be useful, particularly in the introduction and conclusion of a talk, but try to avoid using too many clichés. A well chosen anecdote can add interest to the point you are trying to make.

Write or type out your first draft and read it over and over again making any necessary corrections and amendments.

When you are reasonably satisfied with your draft prepare it in numbered paragraphs under the various headings on sheets of paper no larger than A5 or on postcards. Indent the first line of each new paragraph and make sure you end the paragraph at the bottom of the paper or postcard so that you are not standing before your audience turning pages over and losing the thread of what you are saying. The following illustrates these points—

MR. CHAIRMAN, LADIES AND GENTLEMEN,

1. **I CONSIDER** IT A GREAT HONOUR TO BE INVITED TO RESPOND TO THE TOAST TO THE GUESTS . . . AND ON MY OWN BEHALF AND ON BEHALF OF YOUR OTHER GUESTS . . . I WOULD LIKE TO THANK YOU MOST SINCERELY FOR THE KIND THINGS WHICH HAVE BEEN SAID ABOUT US . . . AND FOR THE WARMTH AND SINCERITY WITH WHICH THIS TOAST HAS BEEN RECEIVED.

2. **FOR MY PART** . . . THE ROYAL NAVY IS VERY DEAR TO MY HEART . . . AND I AM ALWAYS THRILLED TO HAVE THE OPPORTUNITY OF MEETING THOSE WHO MAINTAIN ITS HIGH TRADITIONS OF SERVICE . . .

3. **WE ARE** BY HERITAGE A SEAFARING NATION . . . AND FROM THE WOODEN WALLS OF DRAKE TO THE LATEST NUCLEAR POWERED SUBMARINE OF TODAY . . . OUR NAVY HAS BEEN OUR GREATEST NATIONAL PRIDE . . . A PRIDE WHICH I PERSONALLY SHARE TO THE FULL.

4. **WHEN I CONSIDER** THAT I AM MAKING THIS RESPONSE ON BEHALF OF THE OTHER PRINCIPAL GUESTS HERE TONIGHT . . . INCLUDING TWO OF OUR NAVAL COMMANDERS, I REALISE WHY THE NAVY HAS COME TO BE KNOWN AS THE SILENT SERVICE . . . THEY ARE BEING TRUE TO THEIR SERVICE TONIGHT BY REMAINING SILENT AND LETTING ME GET ON WITH THE BUSINESS OF RESPONDING TO THE TOAST.

5. **MR CHAIRMAN** . . . I KNOW I SPEAK FOR ALL YOUR GUESTS WHEN I SAY THANK YOU FOR YOUR SPLENDID HOSPITALITY . . . AND FOR YOUR GOOD-WILL WHICH WE WARMLY RECIPROCATE.

If your notes have to be handwritten then write them in block capitals for even your own handwriting can become indecipherable if you are feeling a little nervous. If type-written, prepare the notes in capitals with a new ribbon in the machine to obtain a bold typeface, because you can find yourself in a hall where the lighting is dim and you may have forgotten your spectacles.

(*iv*) Having prepared your speech on small sheets of paper or cards it is time to rehearse it over and over again. Invite your family or some long-suffering friend to act as a sounding board and rehearse standing before a mirror to ensure that you look as good as you sound.

(*v*) When the all-important day arrives and you stand before your audience, remember Cicero's advice that your speech should be delivered with dignity and grace.

First impressions are always important so take care in selecting a smart but comfortable outfit in keeping with the occasion.

Once you have arrived at the place where you are to make your address be sure to visit the cloakroom and examine your appearance in a mirror to make sure you are looking your best.

If you are to deliver your speech from a platform as you take your place with the Chairman and any others who are to make up the platform party, make a slow, sure-footed entrance. Once in position on the platform you will no doubt sit for the Chairman's opening speech. Sit comfortably but do not slouch. Be sure to make a point of glancing at the Chairman during his introductory remarks and try to smile and appear at ease, even if you are hoping that the floorboards will open up and swallow you!

When you are on your feet ready to address your audience, stand comfortably, with your weight equally apportioned on both feet and remember not to fidget or to slump in any way. The man who has a habit of standing with one hand in his trouser pocket should make a determined effort to avoid that stance when speaking to an audience for it conveys the impression he could not care less about the people he is addressing.

(*vi*) Brevity. The late King Albert of the Belgians was often heard to comment to his

Aides, "Let us be brief, for the sake of those who are going to listen to us".

6. AFTER DINNER SPEAKING

There is a rare breed of person who has a natural talent for making a first class after dinner speech, the kind of speech that turns a moderately pleasant function into a most enjoyable evening. Should the speaker be something of a raconteur as well, this gives added sparkle to the occasion but alas, these gifted people are all too few.

If you are one of the many not so richly endowed and you have been asked to speak at a celebration dinner or some such social function, there are one or two golden rules to keep uppermost in your mind. First, your speech should be sincere yet light-hearted for people do not go to a social function to listen to serious speeches, nor to hear a speaker talking "shop". Secondly, but equally as important, be brief. If there is to be dancing or an entertainment to follow, you can be sure the guests will be thinking ahead in anticipation rather than concentrating on your speech.

Try to introduce some humour but avoid any story which could give offence in any way, especially in mixed company.

Should you have the misfortune to speak following one of those unmitigating bores, intoxicated by the sound of his or her own voice, who goes droning on, oblivious of the exasperation created, make sure you get your speech over in as short a time as possible, even if it means cutting out some of your best phrased platitudes. If, when you get up, you find one or two guests are discreetly leaving the table and making for the cloakroom (or bar) and others showing signs of restlessness by fidgeting with the table appointments, wind up your speech as quickly as possible.

For well over half a century the late Lord Boothby was famed as a raconteur and often told the story of how, as a young man entering politics, he was taken to a dinner in the House of Lords by F. E. Smith, who later became Lork Birkenhead. A famous elder statesman, well known for his long boring speeches, was taking even longer and proving to be even more boring than usual that night. Many of the diners were nodding off when F. E. Smith scribbled a message on a scrap of paper, folded it and beckoned a waiter who was then seen to position himself behind the speaker and adroitly place the paper in the speaker's hand. The speaker glanced down at the paper and immediately sat down, much to the relief of all present. As they left the House of Lords, Lord Boothby asked Smith what was contained in the message sent to the speaker. The reply came, "Your trouser buttons are undone".

Examples of short speeches suitable for gatherings where there is to be a display or dancing to round off the evening entertainment are set-out in Appendix A on pages 153-164 *post*).

7. GIVING AN ADDRESS

If you accept an invitation to talk to a group of people about a subject in which you specialise or are particularly well versed, it can be assumed your audience has chosen to be present to listen to you and will give you a fair hearing.

Be sure to enquire how long you are expected to speak and try not to exceed the time stated. When preparing your speech ensure that the salient points are reached at an early stage otherwise you could arrive at the vital part of your address and find some of your audience have to leave to catch their train or bus.

After careful thought and adequate preparation you will perhaps present your address by reading from papers but this method has one great pitfall for the novice speaker and it is one into which many specialists can also fall. This is, reading page after page without changing the tone of voice or putting any expression into what is being read; the result being a very dull and uninteresting experience for the audience no matter how informative the address set out to be.

The thing to remember is that you are not reading aloud to yourself but trying to pass on your knowledge to others. To capture the interest of your audience you must vary your tone of voice and the tempo of your reading. When you come to the end of a paragraph or section of your address, pause and look up from your paper and survey your audience. Not only does this make your audience feel at one with you, particularly if you catch them by the eye, but you can judge the amount of interest you are creating.

Prince Charles has very wisely advised that if you see a glazed look come over the face of your audience, it is time to change the theme and introduce some humour.

8. SHORT SOCIAL SPEECHES

There are many social occasions when a speech need be not more than a few well chosen sentences, especially if the audience is standing up, as at a bazaar or fête, although as with all speeches if the event is to go well what is said needs to be carefully thought out and prepared beforehand. For such an occasion, if may not be necessary to carry the full text of the speech but last minute panic could be avoided and confidence ensured by having the headings of each paragraph typed in capitals or hand printed in capitals on a small card not much larger than a visiting card, which could be held in the palm of the hand and glanced at before the commencement of the speech.

Set out in Appendix A(e) on page 163 *post* is an example of such a speech, followed by the headings which could act as an aide-memoirc.

9. TAKING THE CHAIR

The success or failure of a meeting can depend to a large extent on the person who occupies the chair, although it is not essential for that person to be a gifted speaker.

It is the duty of the person taking the chair (addressed as "Mr. Chairman" or "Madam Chairman") to conduct the business of the meeting and ensure that everyone present is given the opportunity of taking such part in the meeting as may be permissible by the rules and regulations governing the body. A civic leader presiding over a meeting of a local authority conducts the meeting in accordance with the standing orders of the authority and any overriding Acts of Parliament which affect it.

A company chairman looks for his authority to the Companies Acts and to the Memorandum and Articles of Association of the company itself.

On the occasion of the annual general meeting of the works sports club or the local philanthropic society, or similar organisation, it should be the duty of the person taking the chair to conduct the business of the meeting and to maintain strict impartiality at all times. If there are two schools of thought on any matter under consideration, it is up to the person occupying the chair to make sure that both sides are given a fair hearing, no matter what his or her own personal views might be.

Where a guest speaker has been invited to address a meeting, the person occupying the chair should be at great pains to make sure he or she does not steal the speaker's subject. How many times have we heard the well-worn cliché, "Your Chairman has already told you . . ."?

The success of a social gathering can best be assured if the person presiding is a cheerful sociable person with an easy manner, who takes the trouble to become cognisant with the names and background of the principal guests before the event. In fact, the person presiding at a social gathering is acting as host or hostess and should be at pains to make sure that everyone present at the party has an enjoyable time.

10. VOTES OF THANKS

The days of the long drawn out meetings are over and there are fewer great orators in our midst than in the past. Would it not therefore be a good idea for organisations to leave any vote of thanks to a single speaker rather than have a proposer and seconder? It often seems so pointless and dreary to have one member rise to his feet and say, "Mr. Chairman, Ladies and Gentlemen, there is nothing I can say that Mr. . . . has not already said when proposing this vote of thanks to our speaker. I therefore have pleasure in seconding it."

The occasion when a seconder can have a real contribution to make is when there are a majority and minority group making up a body such as a local authority. To have a member of the majority group proposing a vote of thanks, followed by a member of the minority group supporting it, does give the minority members an opportunity of taking part in the proceedings and having their voice heard.

Where there is to be a proposer and seconder, it is a good idea for the two to confer and agree the points each will cover.

11. READING MINUTES

If the first time you speak before an audience the task involves nothing more than reading the minutes of the previous meeting at a works social club, there should be a conscious use of the voice so that it can be heard distinctly by all present and the reading should be at a pace that enables the content of the matter to be fully absorbed by the people listening.

12. MICROPHONES

Should it be necessary for you to use a microphone, it is a good idea to familiarise yourself with its controls and test it thoroughly by having a practice before the important occasion. Public address systems have an unfortunately all-too-frequent habit of cutting out without a speaker noticing the fact, besides their irritating habit of whistling and whining from time to time.

Few speakers would have the presence of mind shown by Sir Winston Churchill on one occasion when he was addressing an audience of thousands in a sports stadium and the microphone faulted. The audience started to call out, "Louder, louder". Immediately Sir Winston realised what had happened he discarded the microphone and roared in a voice which could be heard by all, "Now that we have exhausted the resources of science we shall fall back upon Mother Nature and do our best!" He thundered on and held his audience with him to the last word of his speech.

13. PREPARING SPEECHES FOR OTHERS TO DELIVER

Thoughout my career it was part of my duties to prepare notes and speeches for people taking part in a wide variety of public functions and before varied audiences and groups. In the early days I evolved a practice of familiarising myself with their own particular, if not peculiar, vernacular and have found that this can be most successful for helping speakers who have little time for preparing their own speeches.

To do this I tried to get to know the person who was to make the speech and studied his or her mannerisms; I made a point of engaging them in conversation in order to memorise their pet phrases and to be able to judge the extent of their vocabulary. Bearing all this in mind, I then selected phrases for the speeches I prepared for them to deliver and incorporated their turn of phraseology wherever possible. I found that when a speaker came to deliver the speech, he or she felt more confident with a text tailored to his or her familiar usage, than if trying to cope with more complicated words and phrases. I can recommend this method to any person who is asked to "jot down a few points for me for the annual meeting".

Examples of speeches for social occasions will be found in Appendix A, p. 153 *post*.

Chapter 4
BEHIND THE SCENES

1. THE PRIVATE SECRETARY

The duties of a private secretary are many and varied and call for qualities far beyond the ability to write shorthand rapidly and type accurately. He or she must have a genuine interest in the work they are engaged upon and a feeling that it is worth while and from this will stem the ability to identify himself or herself with the work of the employer.

Many famous people have had cause to give praise to their private secretaries for the invaluable help they have received from them, one such being Lord Asquith, who when he was Chancellor of the Exchequer had as his Private Secretary a young man who later distinguished himself and became well known as Lord Bradbury. During the time he was working for Lord Asquith, Bradbury acquired a deep understanding and sensitive mastery of Lord Asquith's style of letter writing and used it to successs when drafting letters for the Chancellor.

On one occasion he presented Lord Asquith with a particularly good one and earned from him the comment, "Bradbury, when I sign letters I have written myself I sometimes doubt their authenticity, but when I sign letters you have drafted for me such a doubt never crosses my mind", and so it is that good secretaries must be able, with sympathy and imagination to project themselves into the minds of their employers.

Besides dealing with correspondence and keeping an employer's diary up to date, a private secretary will often be called upon to collect data in connection with any invitations the employer accepts. For instance, if a Director of a brewery accepts an invitation from the Licensed Victuallers to attend their annual dinner and propose a toast to the Victuallers' Association, he will find it helpful to know the number of members making up the association, the date it was formed and any notable achievements brought about by the organisation.

The writer Kirkland Bridge once wrote that, ". . . secretaries are the patron saints of all the people who work behind the scenes."

2. THE HONORARY SECRETARY AND ORGANISER

Much valuable work is performed by the honorary secretaries of countless numbers of organisations and groups throughout the length and breadth of the country, a great deal of it being carried out without payment of any kind.

At the peak time for annual meetings, dinners and other social activities organised by charitable and social organisations, there are many letters to write, menus and toast lists to arrange and a thousand and one small details to be attended to if the occasion is to pass off without a hitch—and what secretary would have it otherwise?

During my working life I was responsible for organising many functions each year, ranging from visits by members of the Royal Family to tea parties for a handful of guests. Early on I devised a simple way of making sure that, as far as possible, no detail in connection with the arrangements was overlooked and I would like to suggest to any secretary or organiser, that unless he or she has a more foolproof way of keeping check on day-to-day developments for their functions, they adopt this method.

I might add that even now in my more leisured days of retirement, I still use this method of keeping check on arrangements for our village church fêtes and jumble sales.

At the start I prepare a folder or file for the correspondence, on the inset of which I attach a sheet of ruled paper which I head with the description of the function. Below the heading on the left hand side I set out the details decided upon, such as date, times, venue, catering arrangements, etc. As the plans proceed I enter each development on the appropriate line so that I can see at a glance how the arrangements are progressing and what further action needs to be taken. Three examples are set out on the following pages.

BEES SPORTS CLUB ANNUAL DINNER DANCE

Friday 1st May 1987   Reception 7 to 7.30 pm   Dinner 7.35 to 8.30 pm

                         Speeches 8.30 to 9 pm   Dancing 9 pm to 12 mn

Venue: Grand Hotel Banqueting Hall   Booked *Letter 22/4/86 Confirmed 27/4/86*

Fee for Hall and resident orchestra   *£750*

Menu agreed with Chairman and Hotel Manager *Menu B*   Cost of Meal: *£6.50*

Master of Ceremonies   *Robert Dean. Fee £75. Letter 2/5/86*

Tickets   *£15 ea.*   Maximum no. *200*

Guests	Date Invitations sent	Reply
Mayor and Mayoress	*6/1/87*	*Accepted 10/1/87*
President and wife	*22/4/86*	*Accepted 6/5/86*
Managing Director and lady	*"*	*" 8/5/86*
Company Chairman and wife	*"*	*" 14/5/86*
Company Secretary and wife	*"*	*" 9/5/86*

Toast List	Letter sent	Reply
The Queen Proposed by the President	*22/4/86*	*✓ 6/5/86*

The Bees Sports Club
  Proposed by The Mayor
  Response by the President
	6/1/87
	22/4/86
		✓ 10/1/87
		✓ 6/5/86

Our Guests
  Proposed by The Chairman
  Response by The Managing
    Director Bees Ltd.,
	22/4/86
	22/4/86
		✓ 14/5/86
		✓ 8/5/86

Draft ticket to Printer   *6/1/87*   Proof recd.   *14/1/87*   Checked and retd. *16/1/87*

Tickets from Printer   *24/1/87*   Tickets to members as per list   *23/4/87*

Draft Menu and Toast List
  to Printer   *31/3/87*   Proof recd.   *8/4/87*   Checked and retd. *10/4/87*

Menu and Toast List recd.
  from Printer   *28/4/87*   To Hotel   *30/4/87*

Flowers for ladies ordered   – *17/4/87*

THE HONORARY SECRETARY AND ORGANISER

ANNUAL GENERAL MEETING OF THE BEES SPORTS CLUB

FRIDAY 17th April 1987

Venue: The Club House   Time: 7.30 pm

Steward informed   *letter* 22/4/86

Draft Agenda to Chairman   2/2/87

Draft invitation to Printer   6/2/87

Proof from Printer   19/2/87   Checked and retd.   20/2/87

Invitations from Printer   27/2/87   Sent to members   25/3/87

Letters of invitation to special guests —   Reply received

   The Mayor   *letter* 2/2/87   *acceptance* 6/2/87

   The President   "   "   "   10/2/87

   Managing Director   "   "   *Unable to accept*

   Chairman of Board   "   "   *acceptance* 17/2/87

   Company Secretary   "   "   "   19/2/87

Advert. in local paper sent   6/4/87   for issue on   10/4/87

HEPTONSTALL PARISH CHURCH

  JUMBLE SALE   CHURCH HALL   FRIDAY 20th FEBRUARY 1987

Doors open   6.30 pm   Setting up from 2.30 pm

Hall booked   14/1/87

Admission   10p.

Posters run off   4/2/87   Distributed   5/2/87

Refreshments — tea and biscuits 20p. — *Gill, Lilian & Jessie*

Doorkeeper   *The Vicar*

Helpers —   *Ann H.*   *Christine*
         Adrienne   *Barbara*
         Ethel   *Myra*
         Ronda   *Fred*
         Bessie   *Jim*

Advert. sent to H.B. Times   13/2/87   for issue   20/2/87

Clearance of left overs   *Mr Potter. H 56328   8.30 pm 20/2/87*

3. THE TELEPHONE

Although we all find the telephone a great boon, it is inadvisable to depend entirely on telephone conversations when making arrangements for any detail in connection with the organisation of a function—no matter how trivial it may be. By all means use the telephone to get over the detailed points but confirm it in writing later so that there can be no question of misunderstanding or someone having misheard.

4. THE ANNUAL MEETING

Although your committee will no doubt have decided on the guest speaker and the form the meeting is to take, and past practice will determine this to some extent, it is up to the secretary to make sure that the guest speaker is supplied with full background details of the organisation, i.e. the aims and objects of the organisation, size of its membership, the number of people estimated to be present at the meeting, and—most important of all—the length of time the speaker is expected to address the meeting.

Nothing can be more frustrating to a speaker than to prepare a half hour address and arrive at a meeting only to be told in a most charming but off-hand manner, "Oh, our speakers in the past have only taken about ten minutes". And it does happen!

There are occasions when a civic head has been invited to preside over the annual general meeting of a local organisation but there is a good deal to be said for the alternate method of having the active President or Chairman of the organisation preside over the business of the meeting as he will no doubt have carried through the work of the year under review and be familiar with all the details to be reported on.

By all means invite the civic head to open the proceedings and give the meeting a civic blessing, as it were, for this gives the Lord Mayor, Mayor or Council Chairman the opportunity not only of identifying the local authority with the various groups making up the community but of offering thanks on behalf of the area, to those who, year in and year out, carry on a great deal of commendable work on behalf of a multitude of good causes.

Since local government re-organisation and the creation of much larger authorities, civic heads, like most people involved in public affairs, face an expanding and taxing number of calls on their time and after opening a meeting and greeting those present, he or she would then be able to move on to fulfil another engagement.

The secretary should make sure that all who are on the platform or are to take any part in the proceedings, receive a copy of the agenda or programme prior to the meeting.

5. ELECTION OF PRESIDENT, PATRON, ETC.

The majority of local organisations, be they charitable, social or sporting, choose to elect a "name" to grace their body as President or Patron. In most cases, the organisation has a hard working Chairman and the President or Patron is expected to do little other than lend the dignity of his name to the official notepaper, present himself and his good lady at the Annual Dinner and at the Annual Meeting present or send along his donation towards the funds, coupled with his personal thanks to those who have relieved him of so much hard work during the past year, together with his best wishes for the coming year.

Some organisations seek to extend this source of income by inviting a number of other people known to be interested in their work but not actively associated with the organisation, to act as Vice-Presidents or Vice-Patrons, sometimes for a fixed fee.

A word of warning here to organisations who decide to invite their civic leader to support them in this way. As has been stated in other parts of this book, the civic head, be he Lord Mayor, Mayor, or Chairman of the Council, has precedence in all places in his area and it would not be in accordance with that precedence for him to accept office as Vice-President or Vice-Patron of a local group having as its President or Patron another local dignitary.

If the town cricket club have been given a cricket ground by a wealthy local business man, the Club Committee might rightly feel that the donor's generosity should be acknowledged and they might invite him to act as President but at the same time they also wish to have their civic head associated with the Club. In such a case it would be correct to create the office of Honorary President for the civic head,

66

but it would be inappropriate to invite him to act as Vice-President to the local business man.

When issuing an invitation of this kind, try to avoid the tactless point made by the honorary secretary of an old people's organisation who wrote to his local Mayor inviting him to act as President of the organisation, ". . . as your predecessors have done. We hope you will be able to accept because we have a stock of notepaper headed—President—His Worship the Mayor, and we want to use it up".

6. THE ANNUAL DINNER AND TOAST LIST

After reserving the room, sorting out the menu with the caterers, arranging for the necessary printing, etc., there will be the task of settling the toast list.

Again it is advisable to follow up any verbal requests in writing clearly stating what is expected of the speaker. There have been occasions where guests have arrived at functions and unexpectedly found themselves on the list of speakers. This is clearly unsatisfactory. No matter how small the gathering it is advisable that a speaker be given advance notice of what is expected of him or her.

If writing to invite a well known sportsman to attend the annual dinner of your sports club and propose what will probably be the main toast of the evening, be sure to let him know the exact style in which the toast will appear on the toast list, for example, "The Bee's Sports and Social Club", the name of the person who will be responding and his connection with the Club (he will no doubt be the President or Chairman of the Club), where the toast appears on the toast list and the length of time he is expected to speak, together with some background data on the club, if he is not familiar with it.

When inviting a guest to respond to the toast to "The Guests" be sure to supply a list of other guests on whose behalf the response is to be made.

It will be found that principal guests and speakers appreciate information on such points as the following, where they are applicable to the type of function you are organising—

The exact nature of the function, *i.e.*, Annual Dinner or Annual Dinner and Dance, etc.

Where it is to be held (with a map if an out of town guest, or if the function is to be held in the London area).

Day and date.

Who is to preside.

Time of commencement of—
(*a*) Reception (if there is to be one).
(*b*) Dinner or other function.

Exactly who is to be invited (that is, speaker and wife, or in the case of a single sex gathering—just the speaker).

Name of toast or subject of speech required, and the length of time allotted for speech.

Dress to be worn.

Approximate time of conclusion of function.

6. LOYAL TOASTS

Where there are to be toasts following a meal, it is the accepted custom that the first toast is to The Queen. At banquets where there is a Member of the Royal Family present and at more formal ceremonial functions it is customary to include the second Loyal Toast. The form approved by The Queen for these Loyal Toasts is as follows—

1. The Queen
2. Queen Elizabeth the Queen Mother, the Prince Philip, Duke of Edinburgh, the Prince and Princess of Wales, and other members of the Royal Family.

In the County of Lancashire where the Sovereign is also Duke of Lancaster, or at functions arranged by Lancastrian organisations, the first of the Loyal Toasts is proposed in the following form—

The Queen, Duke of Lancaster.

In Britain we have a centuries old custom that guests do not smoke until immediately after coffee is served and the Loyal Toasts are given. Not all overseas guests, especially Americans, are willing to forego their cigars or cigarettes for the time required for the full meal and for this reason the Loyal Toast is sometimes proposed after the main course. Although this practice no doubt pleases those who are smokers,

69

it does mean that the non-smokers have to endure other people's cigar and cigarette smoke and smells along with their dessert.

The Prince of Wales championed our age-old tradition over trend at the Lord's Taverners Silver Jubilee dinner in London and refused to propose the Loyal Toast immediately after the main course.

The Chairman or toastmaster at a function usually announces immediately after the Loyal Toasts, "Ladies and Gentlemen, you may now smoke", or less formally but very pointedly "Ladies and gentlemen, if you must, you may".

8. OTHER TOASTS

Most people attending a dinner, banquet, ladies festival or whatever title is chosen for a gathering, regard it as a form of celebration and spend time, effort and money in preparation for the event. Should the function prove to be dull and boring all this effort is wasted and for this reason organisers should take care in deciding upon the number of toasts to follow the Loyal Toast and the selection of speakers.

We all know that nothing kills a party quicker than boring speakers whereas a witty, crisply delivered speech can create just the right atmosphere for making the occasion enjoyable for all present.

No doubt learning from the past, some wise organisers now make a polite request to speakers to keep within a fixed time limit. This should apply to all who are to speak, excepting perhaps where a very distinguished speaker is invited and the function has been arranged for the sole purpose of hearing such a speaker.

Organisers should try to select speakers of widely differing personalities and if they feel they have to let "old so-and-so who is such a pompous crushing bore" respond to the toast to the Club because he is the backbone of the organisation and looks forward to speaking at the annual dinner, then for goodness sake search hard to make sure he is followed by a light-hearted witty speaker, preferably an attractive female.

The late Lord Birkett was fond of relating the story of how, as Chairman of the Court of London University, he was asked to recommend the name of a guest speaker—the only qualification being that he had to be a wit. "I am sorry", replied Lord Birkett, "I cannot find you a wit, so I enclose the names of two half-wits".

9. ORGANISING A DANCE OR SOCIAL EVENT

When the exact form has been decided upon and the reservation of accommodation made, the band booked, master of ceremonies appointed, programme drawn up, flowers ordered, special guests invited (and all confirmed in writing), the printing of tickets put in hand as well as publicity planned, if this is to be a public function, or invitations sent if a private one, the organising secretary then has to make sure that a day to day check is maintained on the number of acceptances or tickets sold, as the case may be, in order that the Home Office regulations regarding permitted numbers for the safety of the building are not violated (these should be ascertained when reserving the accommodation), and of course, to keep the caterer alive to requirements.

10. MEETING SPECIAL GUESTS

It is most important that principal guests and speakers be met on arrival and some officer or member of the organisation should be deputed to await the arrival of the civic heads, speakers and other special guests and conduct them to the cloak-room and then on to the President or Chairman of the organisation.

Be sure to reserve car parking spaces for your special guests and let them know that this has been done.

On leaving the function special guests should be escorted to their cars.

11. CLOAKROOMS

All kinds of halls and rooms are used for gatherings of every description, some having cloakrooms and toilets clearly indicated. Where this is not so, it is a good idea for the organiser to make sure that notices are displayed in prominent positions for all to see.

12. ARRANGING THE TOP TABLE OR PLATFORM PARTY

The first point to be decided upon is—who is to preside over the gathering? In most cases, the President or Chairman presides and he occupies the central position. If the civic head is present then he takes precedence over all other guests, excepting the Lord Lieutenant of the County. The civic head is therefore placed on the immediate right of the Chairman, with his lady being on the immediate left of the Chairman, or on the right of her own husband.

If at the annual dinner of the local football club, the Mayor is to propose the toast to the Club and the Captain of England is present as a special guest to respond to the toast to "The Guests", then it would be in order to place the Mayor on the immediate right of the Chairman of the Football Club who would be presiding, with the Mayoress on the Mayor's right and the Captain of England on the Chairman's immediate left, so giving the Chairman the opportunity of dividing his time between two such important guests.

13. ISSUING INVITATIONS

When inviting a guest in a representative capacity the office held should be indicated on the invitation, for example—

> The President of the Blank Rotary Club (Mr. William White, J.P.) and Mrs. White.

(If the function is to be a mixed one and your principal guest is married, be sure to invite the other half.)

A bachelor being invited to a mixed gathering should receive an invitation addressed to—

Mr John Brown and Lady.

73

This form should also be used if you are unable to ascertain a gentleman's marital status.

When inviting a single woman to a mixed gathering the words "and Partner" or "and Escort" follow her name—

Miss Mary Brown and Partner.

A widow should be addressed by her late husband's christian name—

Mrs John Black and Escort.

A woman who has been divorced is addressed by her own christian name, as in the following example—

Mrs Helen Black and Escort.

When sending out invitations, bearing in mind the cost of postal services nowadays, it is a good idea to state on the invitation card "Unless a reply is received by .... (indicate a certain date) it will be assumed you are unable to accept", or "Please reply only if you can attend", or some such wording.

14. WRITING LETTERS

There is much to be said for the modern trend towards doing away with the stilted verbiage of old style letter writing. The important thing to bear in mind when writing official letters is to be as courteous as possible without being too ingratiating and simply and directly state what has to be stated, without discarding too many of the formalities.

For instance, if the Mayor is personally known to the writer of a letter seeking to invite him to officiate at some local gathering, the writer should bear in mind that it is the Mayor in office who is being invited, not "Bob" or "Tom" as he is known to the writer when chatting over the garden wall. The salutation on the letter should therefore be "Dear Mr. Mayor", so giving recognition to his office and indicating that it is in his capacity as Mayor that he is being invited to attend the gathering.

An example of the old style is shewn in the following letter—

"Dear Mr. Mayor,

School Prize-giving
Wednesday, 3rd December 1987
as from 7.30 p.m.

A most cordial invitation is extended to you and the Mayoress to be our Guests of Honour on the above occasion. We should be further honoured if you would kindly consent to open the proceedings and may we ask if the Mayoress would graciously consent to present the prizes.

Full details as to the procedure for the evening, etc., will be sent to you shortly.

Yours respectfully,
HEAD TEACHER."

How much better is the following—

"Dear Mr. Mayor,

On behalf of the School, I have pleasure in inviting you and the Mayoress to our Prize-giving to be held in the School Hall on Wednesday, 3rd December 1987 at 7.30pm. If you are able to come we hope you will agree to say a few words at the commencement and that the Mayoress will present the prizes.

Yours truly,
HEAD TEACHER."

"Mr." or "Esq."

By long established English ruling, the only people entitled to the appellation "Esq." after their names, were members of the leading professions, these being the Church, the Armed Services, the Law and Medicine. All others were addressed by the term "Mr.".

Our current habit of applying "Esq." to all and sundry appears to stem from the lawyers dealing more and more with landed squires as they have found it necessary to sell their land and property. As a result our new land and property owners have been given the benefit of being addressed as "Esq." until it has reached such proportions that it is now very difficult to lay down any kind of ruling on the matter.

Indicative of our present day attitude to materialism is the view that all professional men, millionaires and gentlemen are entitled to the appellation "Esq.". But who defines what constitutes a gentlemen?

One point beyond dispute is that "Mr." should not be used along with "Esq." just as "Messrs." should not be added to the name of a limited company or a firm which does not carry a proper name, for example—

York House Antiques.

15. THE TYPEWRITER

Our present educational system does not include formal lessons in handwriting and perhaps because of this a well typed letter sent on behalf of an organisation gives a rather more favourable impression than one which is handwritten and difficult to read.

Word processors and golf-ball self correcting typewriters used by trained operators produce easy to read correspondence with a pleasing professional finish but not many of the committee members pressed into taking office as honorary secretaries of the smaller community groups are fortunate enough to have access to such expensive pieces of equipment and most have to make do with the discarded office manual machine purchased at a specially low price or a portable which may be a left over from student days.

These short notes are for the guidance of those who have access to the latter, but do not have the benefit of training in the use of the typewriter.

When about to use the machine place it on a table or desk and sit on a chair at a height which will allow your forearms to be on a level with the keyboard. To prevent the machine from slipping when in use, place it on a pad.

In the interests of economy it is advisable to use a one-colour ribbon, turning the ribbon from top to bottom when worn. Be sure to clean the typewriter regularly and have it serviced occasionally by a specialist typewriter firm. Oil the mechanism very sparingly.

Use a soft brush to clear away dust and eraser grit and be sure to clean the keys before starting to type. If you don't have a brush for the keys, a medium toothbrush will serve the purpose and will keep the typeface free from dirt and ribbon ink and prevent the typed article having a blotchy appearance, which is a sure sign of an untrained typist.

Keep the platen clean by wiping it regularly with a soft cloth to which a little methylated spirits has been applied.

Most organisations have notepaper printed with the name of the organisation and details of the honorary officers but if you are using plain paper and typing these details onto the paper, remember that there is a right and wrong side to most papers. Hold a sheet of paper up to the light and almost always you will see the watermark which denotes the right side of the paper. Always make a carbon copy of any letters sent.

If you make a mistake erase the error with one of the several correcting fluids or papers on sale from stationers, following the manufacturers' instructions which will be found on the product's container. Never type one letter on top of the other without first erasing the error—this is an unforgiveable crime for any typist to commit and gives a messy appearance to any typed material.

A study of business letters will give a guide as to how to set out a letter. Try to achieve a balanced look and once you have selected the style which looks right on your notepaper practice will help to produce a reasonable standard.

16. THE PRESS

For good or ill, the press plays an important part in any community and goes a great way towards influencing public opinion.

In recent years local authorities and large industrial undertakings have recognised the need for close co-operation with the press and have appointed press and public relations officers, not only to enable them to better tackle the problem of explaining or selling themselves to the public, but to make sure that as far as possible, facts reported are correct in substance, no matter how the finished article may finally be presented to the reading public—for that is entirely in the hands of the editorial staff.

Miscellaneous news items in the local press giving details of the sports day organised by the works sports club, or the Village Institute's Annual Garden Party opened by the wife of the local Member of Parliament are read by the majority of local residents and it is advisable for the sake of goodwill and future harmony, that the press reports should be correct.

For instance, nothing can be more distressing for Mrs. X. who played the piano for the rendering of the National Anthem at the Garden Party, than to find that every helper but herself is mentioned in the press report the following weekend. Nowhere does her name appear! No matter what the explanation for this omission, it could mean that the honorary secretary of the Village Institute has to find another pianist for next year's Garden Party.

Most local newspapers employ a number of reporters who appear to spend their working life rushing from the scene of the latest local drama to the meeting of the divisional education committee, followed by yet another local gathering, but it is not possible for them to attend each and every function held within the area they cover. In spite of this the editorial staff are almost always willing to publish a brief report of any event which is of local interest, if such a report is supplied to them.

Some organisations have found it advisable to appoint one of their members to act as press officer, others leave their chairman or honorary secretary to deal with this. No matter who undertakes the job, there are a few points to bear in mind, the first being that no matter what information is supplied, the editorial staff alone decide what is published, and so long as the facts are not incorrectly stated, there is absolutely no redress for any misinterpretations that are placed on what eventually appears in the newspapers. Because of this, it is important that any material supplied to the press for publication be written as clearly as possible. Ambiguous phrases which are not instantly understood should be avoided. Wherever possible it is a good thing to supply a typewritten copy in double spaced typing, as handwriting is easily misread, especially so where proper names are concerned. If a typewriter is not available, then print the whole thing rather than run the risk of having an error upset a local dignitary. It will be well worth the extra effort and the newspaper staff will appreciate it and be far more ready to use it.

Another point to remember is that the press will be more co-operative about using your report in full if you keep it brief and to the point.

Even if a reporter does attend a local gathering, it is quite a good idea for the organiser to supply a printed list of the names of persons it is desired should be mentioned. Where speeches are made, the organiser should make sure that the press are seated where they can best hear the speakers. It is also helpful if a copy of the speeches can be made available to the reporters, although this is not always possible.

Co-operation with the press in this way helps to avoid too many of those "Correction" paragraphs at the bottom of columns not normally scanned by the readers of the "Social and Personal Column", and can prevent anything as embarrassing as the occasion when the village squire and his good lady were having their first-born christened and giving her a whole string of family Christian names. Remembering that the local vicar was rather forgetful, they decided to print the names on a card and pin the card on the baby's christening robe. When the ceremony ended a young reporter from the local press enquired from the Irish Nanny the names the child had been given and received the reply, "Pinned on her". The next issue of the local press carried a report of the christening and concluded, "the child was named Pindonna".

17. FUND RAISING

The days of the wealthy benefactor who was the mainstay of his pet society or charity are over—with very few exceptions—and Bob Geldof stands alone as a twentieth century fund raiser extraordinarius. Few of our national charities exist without a full-time paid staff of organisers with some of the large funds employing consultants using high pressure business techniques. By contrast the members of small local groups seeking to raise the few hundred pounds each year which are required to enable the organisation to carry on, are continually trying to find imaginative ways of attracting those funds with sponsored abseiling and other new activities proliferating, yet the well-tried cheese and wine party, the sherry evening, the bingo sessions, the raffle and the draw are still bringing in a welcome source of income for many deserving causes.

For those who are new to fund raising there are certain regulations to bear in mind governing parties for gain where intoxicating liquor is to be served and when arranging a bingo session or a raffle or draw for in some cases a licence or registration is required. For a party involving liquor it may be that the organisation needs to hold an occasional licence under the provisions of The Licensing (Occasional Permissions) Act 1983, application for which must be made to The Clerk to the Justices for the area in which the party is to be held and an early enquiry at that office will assist the organiser. When granted this licence which is valid for one year allows the holders to serve liquor for gain up to four times during the year in which the licence runs. Bingo and a large scale raffle or draw with tickets being sold to the general public require that the organisation must register under the gaming and lotteries regulations and enquiries should be made at the office of the Clerk or Chief Executive of the local authority where help and guidance will be forthcoming.

Flag days, street collections and house to house collections are all subject to licence granted either by the local authority or the police authority although each year certain of our national charities are allocated a date when they are allowed to hold street collections and house to house collections throughout the whole of England and Wales under what are known as a Certificate of Exemption from the requirement to obtain local licences. Instances of this are National Life-Boat day held in March each year and the British Legion's Poppy Appeal each November.

Local organisations wishing to raise funds by means of a flag day or house to house collection require a licence or permission under the street collection regulations or the house to house collection regulations and should seek help from the office of the Clerk or Chief Executive of the Local authority for the area in which it is desired to organise the collection.

18. IN THE NAME OF CHARITY

Much of the legislation which heralded the welfare state as we know it today in our country, built on or took the place of voluntary work started by wealthy philanthropists. In spite of all the state caring there are more than 150,000 charities already in existence in England and Wales at the present time and more are being set up each year. The Charity Commissioners who are responsible for overseeing these organisations are known to lack adequate resources and powers to investigate and supervise all of them.

By their very nature, charities must be run on trust with the public having the right to expect that the money they give is properly spent. For this reason anyone who is approached to assist with fund raising activities should make careful investigation into the standing of the organisation and the people running it before becoming involved with the work.

This is not to say that there is not a great deal of splendid work carried out on behalf of the community by the numerous charity groups at work. Indeed it would be a sorry day for our country if the voluntary caring for the needs of the less fortunate members of our community were to be taken over entirely by the state.

Chapter V

FORMS OF ADDRESS AND LETTERS
AFTER NAMES

1. FORMS OF ADDRESS

Full details of the correct forms of address when
writing and speaking to Members of the Royal Family
are set out in Chapter VI. The following is a list of
accepted forms of address to be used when writing or
speaking to distinguished and professional people.
Any title not included in this list will be found in
"Debrett's Correct Form", compiled and edited by
Patrick Montague-Smith, and published by Kelly's
Directories, Neville House, Eden Street, Kingston-
upon-Thames, Surrey.

TITLED PEOPLE

Dukes
Title . . . . His Grace of the Duke of . . . .
Addressed as . . My Lord Duke
or . . Your Grace.

Marquesses
Title . . . . The Most Honourable the
Marquess of . . . .
Addressed as . . My Lord Marquess.

Earls
Title . . . . The Right Honourable the
Earl of . . . .
Addressed as . . My Lord.

Viscounts

Title .... The Right Honourable the
Viscount ....

Addressed as .. My Lord.

Barons

Title .... The Right Honourable the
Lord ....

Addressed as .. My Lord.

Countesses in their own right

Title .... The Countess of ....

Addressed as .. My Lady.

Baronesses in their own right

Title .... The Baroness ....

Addressed as .. My Lady.

Baronets

Title .... Sir Robert ...., Bt.

Addressed as .. Sir Robert.

Baronets' wives
are addressed
formally as .. Your Ladyship,
or .... Lady ....

Knights Grand Cross, Knights Grand Commanders
and **Knights Commanders** are addressed in the
same way as Baronets, but in writing the appropriate initials (G.C.B., K.C.B., etc.) are appended to
the surname after "Bt." if they are also baronets,
or in place of "Bt." if they are not.

Knights Bachelor

Title .... Sir A................ B...............

Addressed as .. Sir.

The wives of these gentlemen are addressed formally as ..... Your Ladyship,

or .... Lady.

Dames

Dames are appointed to the following Orders—

The Order of the Bath (to which women were admitted for the first time in 1971) on two grades—Dame Grand Cross and Dame Commander, with letters after the name as follows—G.C.B., D.C.B.

The Order of St. Michael and St. George with two grades as above and letters after name as follows—G.C.M.G., D.C.M.G.

The Royal Victorian Order, again with two grades and letters after name as follows—G.C.V.O., D.C.V.O.

The Order of the British Empire again with two grades and letters after name as follows—G.B.E., D.B.E.

Title .... Dame Flora W. .... with appropriate letters,

Addressed as ... Dame Flora.

Where a lady already holding a higher title is granted such an award, the appropriate letters should be appended to her name, *e.g.* "The Countess of W......................, G.C.B.".

Lords Lieutenant of Counties

The Lord Lieutenant is usually a peer or a baronet, but sometimes a commoner. The actual title used in the Letters Patent relating to these appointments is "Her Majesty's Lieutenant of and in the County of ...." and this is the correct title whether the holder of the office be a Peer or a commoner. In recent times the style "Lord Lieutenant of ...." has come into use.

The Prefix "Right Honourable"

By long established custom, those who make up Her Majesty's Most Honourable Privy Council (whose function it is to give advice and counsel) are entitled to the designation "The Right Honourable" and this is an honour held for life. Members of the Cabinet are Privy Counsellors.

Many members of the Privy Council have other titles and this results in the prefix becoming absorbed in other designations, for example a Royal Prince admitted a Privy Counsellor remains "His Royal Highness", a Duke remains "His Grace"; a Marquess is still styled "Most Honourable". The style of all other Peers, whether Privy Counsellors or not, is "Right Honourable", although it is more usual to describe them with the prefix "The Right Honorable". A Privy Counsellor who is not a Peer should be addressed in this way. A Peer below the rank of Marquess who is a Privy Counsellor should be addressed as "The Right Honourable the Lord (or Earl or Viscount) ...., P.C.", or less formally, "The Lord (or Earl or Viscount) ...., P.C.".

The Office of the Privy Council use the spelling "counsellor" for those who "give counsel" although there is nothing mandatory about this and Whitaker's Almanack has been known to use both spellings, i.e. counsellor and councillor.

THE CHURCH OF ENGLAND

The Archbishops of Canterbury and York are always appointed as Privy Counsellors and included in their titles are the words Right Honourable.

Title	The Most Reverend and Right Honourable His Grace the Lord Archbishop of ....
Addressed as	My Lord Archbishop,
or	Your Grace.

The Bishop of London is also a Privy Counsellor and therefore styled—

Title	The Right Reverend and Right Honourable the Lord Bishop of London.
Addressed as ..	My Lord Bishop,
or ..	Dear Bishop.

Other Bishops

Title .... The Right Reverend the
Lord Bishop of ....

Addressed as .. My Lord Bishop,

or .. Dear Bishop.

Dean

Title .... The Very Reverend the
Dean of ....

Addressed as .. Dear Dean.

Provost

Title .... The Very Reverend the
Provost of ....

Addressed as .. Dear Provost.

Archdeacon

Title .... The Venerable the
Archdeacon of ....

Addressed as .. Dear Archdeacon.

Canon

Title .... The Reverend Canon
John N. Davidson

Addressed as .. Dear Canon.

Prebendary

Title .... The Reverend Prebendary
James Taylor

Addressed as .. Dear Prebendary.

Rural Dean

There is no special form of address for the office
of Rural Dean.

Vicar

Title .... The Reverend John Harrison
(note that the Christian
name should be used)

Addressed as ... Dear Vicar,

or .. Dear Mr. Harrison.

Where a clergyman is titled, his spiritual title ranks before his secular title, *e.g.* The Reverend Sir Peter Jones, Bt.,

Addressed as .. Dear Vicar,

or .. Dear Sir Peter.

THE ROMAN CATHOLIC CHURCH

Cardinal

Title .... His Eminence Cardinal ....

If an Arch-
bishop .... His Eminence the Cardinal
Archbishop of ....

Addressed as .. Your Eminence.

Archbishops

Title .... The Most Reverend
Archbishop of ....

Addressed as .. Dear Archbishop.

Bishop

Title .... The Right Reverend the
Bishop of ....

Addressed as .. My Lord Bishop,

or .. Dear Bishop.

Canon

Title ....   The Very Reverend
Canon Bernard McBride.

Addressed as .. Dear Canon McBride.

Priest

Title ....   The Reverend Peter Yates

Addressed as .. Father Yates,

or .. Dear Mr. Yates.

MEMBERS OF PARLIAMENT

If a member of the Cabinet and therefore a Privy Counsellor—

Designation ... The Right Honourable
Thomas J. King, M.P.

Addressed as .. Dear Minister,

or .. Dear Mr. King.

If not a member of the Cabinet or a Privy Counsellor—

Designation ... Cyril Smith, Esq., M.B.E., M.P.

Addressed as .. Dear Mr. Smith.

MEMBERS OF EUROPEAN PARLIAMENT

If of no other rank—

Designation ... Mrs. Sheila Faith, M.E.P.

Addressed as .. Dear Mrs. Faith.

Other Titles as appropriate, e.g.—

Designation ... The Right Honourable
Mrs. Barbara Castle, P.C., M.E.P., B.A.

Addressed as .. Dear Mrs. Castle.

THE JUDICIARY

High Court Judge (male) is knighted on appointment

Title .... The Honourable
                  Mr. Justice Popplewell
Addressed as .. My Lord,
         or .. Your Lordship.

High Court Judge (Lady) is created a Dame on appointment

Title .... The Honourable
                  Mrs. Justice Lane
Addressed as .. My Lady,
         or .. Your Ladyship.

County Court Judge

Title .... His (or Her) Honour
                  Judge Lees
Addressed as .. Your Honour.

JUSTICE OF THE PEACE

When writing to a Justice of the Peace on judicial business it is correct to add the letters "J.P." after the name, as in John Bank, Esq., J.P.

Addressed in Court as "Your Worships" if more than one justice is present, although there is a practice currently used by some of the younger advocates of addressing only the magistrate occupying the chair even when there are other magistrates present adjudicating on the bench.

There are those who argue that the term "Your Worships" is out moded as it stems from the days when the local mayor was chairman of the bench but in the absence of an alternative collective noun for a bench of magistrates it always strikes me as being discourteous on the part of an advocate appearing before a bench and addressing only the Chairman as "Sir" or "Madam" as the case may be. The Chairman's colleagues who are assisting him or her are giving their time and attention to the case and should be recognised as taking part in the deliberations, always remembering that the success or failure of the advocacy will be determined by a collective decision of the justices sitting, not by the chairman alone!

There have been occasions at sittings of Juvenile Panels presided over by women magistrates when young defendants let slip a "Miss" and the inevitable consequence of our multi-racial society has led to more than one woman being addressed as "Memsahib".

UNIVERSITIES

The Chancellor

Title		The Chancellor of the University of Manchester
Addressed as	..	Dear Chancellor,
or	..	Dear Professor Griffiths.

The Vice-Chancellor

Title		The Vice-Chancellor of the University of Manchester
Addressed as	..	Dear Vice-Chancellor,
or	..	Dear Sir Mark.

MEDICAL PROFESSION

Surgeon
Designation　...　Ian Burn, Esq., F.R.C.S.
Addressed as　..　Dear Mister Burn.

Doctors of Medicine in General Practice
Designation　...　Dr. Michael Robinson, B.S.
Addressed as　..　Dear Doctor Robinson.

LOCAL AUTHORITIES

Lord Mayors of London, York, Belfast and Cardiff
The full title of the Lord Mayors of these cities is—
The Right Honourable the Lord Mayor of ....

In speech he is
　addressed as .. My Lord Mayor.
The title of The
　Lady Mayor-
　ess is .... The Lady Mayoress of ....
In speech she is
　addressed as . Lady Mayoress.

Lord Mayors of Birmingham, Bradford, Bristol, Coventry, Kingston-upon-Hull, Leeds, Liverpool, Manchester, Newcastle-upon-Tyne, Norwich, Nottingham, Oxford, Plymouth, Portsmouth, Sheffield, Stoke-on-Trent and Westminster.

Title .... The Right Worshipful the
　　　　　　　　Lord Mayor of ....
Addressed as .. My Lord Mayor.

Royal Boroughs. These comprise the Royal Borough of Kensington and Chelsea, the Royal

95

Borough of Kingston-upon-Thames and the Royal Borough of Windsor and Maidenhead.

The full title of

The Mayor is   The Worshipful the Mayor of the Royal Borough of
....

Addressed as .. Mr. Mayor or Madam Mayor.

Mayors of other cities not having Lord Mayors, and Mayors of the Cinque Ports

Title .... The Right Worshipful the Mayor

Addressed as .. Dear Mr. Mayor or Dear Madam Mayor.

London Mayors

Title .... The Worshipful the Mayor of the London Borough of
....

or .. The Mayor of the London Borough of ....

Addressed as .. Dear Mr. Mayor or Dear Madam Mayor.

Mayors of District Councils having been granted Borough status and towns with charter trustees.

Title .... The Worshipful the Mayor of
....

or .. The Mayor of ....

Addressed as .. Dear Mr. Mayor or Dear Madam Mayor.

Town Mayors of parish councils having resolved to adopt the status of "town council" in which case their chairman is styled "town mayor".

Title .... The Town Mayor of ....
Addressed as .. Dear Mr. Town Mayor or
Dear Madam Town Mayor.

From the middle ages onwards until the coming into effect of The Justice of the Peace Act 1968, English mayors held office, first as Custodians of the Peace and latterly as Magistrates, which accounts for the form of address "Your Worship". Under the provisions of the 1968 Act, ex-officio justices ceased and it is now considered inappropriate to address a mayor as "Your Worship" unless he serves on the Commission and is acting in his judicial capacity.

Mayoress

A mayoress has no special designation, this being purely a complimentary title accorded to the wife or companion of the mayor.

Title .... The Mayoress of ....
Addressed
formally as .. Dear Madam Mayoress
informally as . Dear Mayoress.

Deputy Mayor
Title .... The Deputy Mayor of ....
Addressed as .. Dear Mr. Deputy Mayor.

Council Members
Title .... Councillor Colin Dee
Addressed as .. Dear Councillor Dee.

Honorary Aldermen

The Local Government Act 1972 created a right available to all county, London Borough and district councils to confer the title of "honorary alderman" on a person who has rendered eminent services as a past member of the council but who is no longer a member. It is not appropriate to use the title or this honour excepting within the confines of the local authority conferring the honour, in which event the form of address would be—

Title .... Honorary Alderman Henry High

Addressed as .. Dear Honorary Alderman High.

Female Civic Heads

The status of civic heads has been clearly laid down by Parliament in the London Government Act 1963 and the Local Government Act 1972 but nowhere in the many guide lines dealing with the provisions of these two Acts is there clear direction as to how to address a female holding office as lord mayor, mayor or chairman of an authority.

There are those who argue that to address a woman mayor as "mister" and to refer to her as "His Worship" is like addressing a woman Sovereign as "Sir" and referring to her as "His Majesty". No good reason has ever been given for the practice which some (but by no means all) women mayors or council chairmen have chosen or have been advised to adopt, of using the masculine form. If we follow the general example of the Sovereign then sex is not determined by the office one holds. Having written that, I do not overlook the fact that in one single instance, since the days of Henry IV, the Sovereign, irrespective of sex, on succession to the throne, has assumed the title of Duke of Lancaster!

In the absence of any firm guidance it is for each individual to decide on the form of address she prefers and this varies from year to year and area to area, as the following examples show.

Some years ago when Councillor Mrs. Laura Bowles was taking her seat as Mayor of Tunbridge Wells, she told her colleagues on the Council. "I should like to make a request—a very feminine request. That is, please don't call me Mister, Mayor, or Sir or His Worship or even He. Just call me Madam."

During the municipal year 1975/76, Dame Kathleen Ollerenshaw held office as Lord Mayor of Manchester and she held firmly to the view that the correct address for the holder of that office which was granted by Royal Charter in 1893 should be "Lord Mayor", irrespective of the sex of the person appointed.

That same year, Dame Evelyn Denington, D.B.E., held office as Chairman of the then Greater London Council and asked her colleagues to address her simply as "Chairman".

Dame Mary Donaldson, G.B.E., who was Lord Mayor of London during 1983/84 became so exasperated by people referring to her as Lady Mayoress (and they included a former Lord Mayor), that she asked all who did so to contribute £1 to the funds of the National Society for the Prevention of Cruelty to Children. At the end of her year in office, Dame Mary was able to hand over a handsome sum to the Society's funds, so proving that some people's mistakes can benefit others!

During 1984/85, Mrs. Margaret Kyrle was Mayor of Eastleigh in Hampshire and wrote to the *The Observer* about the problem she experienced in getting people to address her as "The Mayor" or "Madam Mayor". People who enquired were told that she liked to be called "Madam Mayor" as opposed to "Mr. Mayor" but in spite of that she found she was often announced as "The Lady Mayor" and sometimes "The Mayoress".

Small wonder the general public are puzzled as to the right form of address for a female elected as Lord Mayor, Mayor or Council Chairman, as there has never been a clear decision reached on the point. Several years ago the local authority associations discussed the matter but no definite ruling was ever reached. How much simpler it would be for all concerned if the Government department responsible would take it upon itself to issue a simple direction, relying now on the Sex Discrimination Act if nothing more and state the obvious—that the form of address for female civic heads should be the feminine one —that is, My Lady Mayor, Madam Mayor or Madam Chairman. No such problem arose when in 1965, this country's first woman High Court Judge was appointed. The then Lord Chancellor, when announcing the appointment ruled that the new Judge be addressed in court as "My Lady" or "Your Ladyship" and this term is now established practice in legal circles.

Where a female civic head is accompanied by her husband or a male companion when carrying out civic engagements, it should be for the holder of the office to decide on the designation to be used to describe her companion, be it Mayor's Escort, Mayor's Consort or just plain Mr. ....

2. IN WHAT ORDER DO I PLACE LETTERS AFTER NAMES?

Here is the order for placing suffixes after names—

FIRST, Honours and Decorations conferred by The Sovereign; these have their own order of precedence as set out in the table of Orders, Decorations and Medals of the more widely distributed honours on page 136.

SECOND comes J.P. (Justice of the Peace) being an appointment by The Lord Chancellor on behalf of The Queen to the Queen's Commission of the Peace, or Q.C. for Queen's Counsel.

THIRD comes D.L. (Deputy Lieutenant) which is an appointment made by Her Majesty's Lord Lieutenant; or M.P. (Member of Parliament) or M.E.P. (Member of the European Parliament) being a position conferred by the electorate.

FOURTH comes degrees conferred by Universities, followed by Fellowships or Memberships of learned or professional bodies.

An example would be if you were writing to a Justice of the Peace holding a Bachelor of Arts degree who has been honoured by Her Majesty by being created a Member of the Order of the British Empire and has been appointed by the Lord Lieutenant as one of his Deputy Lieutenants, the correct way to place the suffixes would be—

Henry Blank, Esq., M.B.E., J.P., D.L., B.A.

3. LETTERS AFTER NAMES

Some letters appearing after names are easily recognised as the abbreviations for a decoration, honour or university degree but there are many others in use today, mainly connected with professional associations and institutions which are not commonly known. Appendix B sets out a comprehensive list of the well known and not so well known letters placed after names.

It should be noted that many of our universities and institutions granting awards by examintion or specialist experience also present honorary awards to people of distinction without the requirement of examination. In most cases the award carries with it the right to place the letters of the award preceded by the abbreviation Hon. after the name. These awards have not been listed but can readily be identified as the following examples shew—

Hon. A.S.T.A.

look up A.S.T.A. viz. Associate of the Swimming Teachers' Association, therefore Honorary Associate of the Swimming Teachers' Association.

Hon. F.R.A.M.

look up F.R.A.M. viz. Fellow of the Royal Academy of Music therefore Honorary Fellow of the Royal Academy of Music.

Chapter VI
ROYAL OCCASIONS

1. ROYAL IMAGES

The Lord Chamberlain's rules governing the use of photographs, portraits, engravings, effigies and busts of The Queen and other members of the Royal Family for commercial purposes were drawn up in 1982 to avoid unfair exploitation of the Royal Family by commercial organisations for their own advantage and prohibit Royal images being used on the following articles:—

> Medals, Medallions and Coins
> Adhesive Seals (including commercially issued stamps)
> Trade Marks and Designs
> Articles of Dress (but not textiles in West African countries)
> Household Linen and Furnishing Fabrics
> Any case, container, box, cover or label.

Should the image of The Queen or a member of the Royal Family be shown with that of another person who is not a member of the Royal Family, the Lord Chamberlain's Office should be approached in writing for permission to use such a picture. Letters should be addressed to—The Lord Chamberlain, St. James's Palace, London, S.W.1.

Images of members of the Royal Family under the age of 18 may not be used for any commercial purpose.

Other than as outlined above, Royal Images may be used only on articles for sale that are of a permanent kind, free from advertisement, in good taste and carry no implication that the firm concerned has received Royal Custom or that the article has been purchased by a member of the Royal Family.

Royal Images may be used for the following articles of stationery provided they are free from advertisement:—

> Portrait prints
> Picture postcards (which may include younger members of the Royal Family in family groups)
> Greetings cards that carry only formal greetings
> Calendars (as a special exception Trade Calendars may carry the name of the firm and its trading description).

Except when advertising a book, newspaper, magazine article or a television documentary about a member of the Royal Family, Royal Images may NOT be used for advertising purposes in any medium.

A firm's advertisement may not include photographs of members of the Royal Family visiting their works or exhibition stands or being publicly involved with their products. Publication of film or photographs of such visits may, however, be used for House Journals or for specifically in-house purposes.

105

Any question of copyright involved in the reproduction of a Royal Image must be settled by the prospective user direct with the copy-right holder.

Certain of these rules are relaxed for National occasions, such as a Royal engagement or a Royal wedding, when the Lord Chamberlain's Office will give due notice in the Press.

2. PERSONAL COMMUNICATION WITH ROYALTY

Royal Ladies of every degree are addressed as "Ma'am". Ma'am is pronounced to rhyme with jam, but with a slightly longer "a". **Not** Madam.

It is always for the Royal Personage to speak first, and it is not customary to address a direct question to a member of the Royal Family. If conversation is more than of the shortest kind, the words "Your Majesty" or "Your Royal Highness" should be introduced.

Pronouns are not used. For example—instead of "I hope you will enjoy this visit to . . ." it should be, "I hope Your Majesty will enjoy this visit to . . .".

Immediately personal notice is made, there should be a curtsy on the part of a woman and a bow from the neck on the part of a man. Men in uniform should, if appropriate to their service or organisation, salute without bowing. Women in uniform, where appropriate, should salute. The curtsy should be made with the body erect, the left foot being placed

106

slightly behind the right foot in order to maintain a good balance, then the left knee goes down about half way between the calf and the ankle of the right leg. For younger members of the Royal Family, the curtsy need not be so deep.

Members of the Royal Family invariably shake hands with those presented to them. When this happens one makes a curtsy as the hand is extended, just touching it at the same time. Men should remove their gloves before shaking hands with Royalty.

As far as women are concerned, the Comptroller in the Lord Chamberlain's Office suggests that they should be guided by the Royal Visitor. If the Royal Visitor is wearing gloves then they cannot be incorrect keeping both hands covered, whereas if the Royal Visitor is not wearing gloves, they too could have both hands uncovered.

If conversation takes place, at the end of the conversation with Royalty, a second curtsy or bow is made and one takes two steps backwards.

It is customary for women to curtsy and men to bow when The Queen and The Queen Mother enter and leave a room although this need not be so deep a curtsy as when being presented.

Other members of the Royal Family to whom a curtsy should be made are The Duke of Edinburgh; The Prince and Princess of Wales; The Duke and Duchess of York; The Prince Edward; The Princess Royal; The Princess Margaret; Princess Alice, Duchess of Gloucester; The Duke and Duchess of

Gloucester; The Duke and Duchess of Kent; Princess Alexandra and Prince and Princess Michael of Kent.

The Princess of Wales; The Duchess of York; The Princess Royal; The Princess Margaret; Princess Alice, Duchess of Gloucester; The Duchess of Gloucester; The Duchess of Kent; Princess Alexandra and Princess Michael of Kent are addressed as "Your Royal Highness", followed by "Ma'am" at a later stage in a conversation.

The Duke of Edinburgh; The Prince of Wales; The Duke of York; The Prince Edward; The Dukes of Gloucester and Kent and Prince Michael of Kent are addressed as "Your Royal Highness" and "Sir" after that.

Some time ago when The Duke of Edinburgh made an extensive tour of Greater London Youth Centres to see for himself the young people in training for his Award Scheme, the Award Office requested that His Royal Highness be addressed as "Sir" on all occasions (not "Your Royal Highness"). No doubt this was due to a desire on the part of His Royal Highness to meet as many young people as possible in the time available to him.

Captain Mark Phillips and Mr. Angus Ogilvy are addressed as "Sir".

When the Queen and the Duke of Edinburgh attend a small luncheon or dinner party, the Queen enters the dining room first accompanied by her host, followed by the Duke of Edinburgh with the hostess. At a luncheon or dinner party of any size, in order that the Royal guests should not be kept waiting whilst all the other guests find their places, Her Majesty enters last, escorted by her host. At the table the Queen sits on the right of the host and the Duke on the hostess's right.

Whenever a member of the Royal Family is present at a gathering, other guests do not leave until the Royal Visitor has been escorted from the hall.

When Royal Ladies are present at a Ball, a gentleman does not ask the Royal Lady to dance unless he has been presented to her, in which event the correct way to ask would be to say, "Ma'am, may I have the honour of this dance".

It is well known that members of the Royal Family, particularly the Royal Ladies, have a natural flair for making people feel at ease.

The following story emanates from the Manchester Diocese of the Church of England so could prove to be apocryphal! It concerns a Royal visit to the north when The Queen was attending a Civic Reception and the Mayoress of the Borough in whose Town Hall the Reception was being held, was engaged in earnest conversation with The Queen and ended a sentence with, "Your Majesty". She then hesitatingly asked, "Is that right or should I call you Ma'am?" to which The Queen is alleged to have replied, "Either is quite acceptable, but don't worry, you have called me 'luv' three times already".

3. INVITATIONS TO MEMBERS OF THE ROYAL FAMILY

Local authorities wishing to extend invitations to members of the Royal Family will no doubt find it appropriate to make the initial approach through the Lord Lieutenant of their County. Many of the large industrial combines and quite a few of the national charities have their own methods of extending invitations, often through one of their Directors. For the smaller organisation seeking to extend an invitation to a member of the Royal Family, the following information may prove helpful.

In all cases the letter of invitation should be addressed to the Private Secretary of the appropriate Royal Household and just as when speaking to a member of the Royal Family pronouns are not used, nor are they in writing.

An invitation to Her Majesty The Queen

The letter should be addressed to—

> The Private Secretary to Her Majesty The Queen,
> Buckingham Palace,
> LONDON, S.W.1.

using the salutation "Sir" or "Dear Sir" with phrases such as "extend an invitation to Her Majesty to perform the opening of our new Headquarters. We very much hope The Queen will agree to honour our Assocation in this way".

An invitation to H.R.H. The Prince Philip, Duke of Edinburgh

The letter should be sent to—

> The Private Secretary to H.R.H. The Prince Philip,
> Buckingham Palace,
> LONDON, S.W.1.

with the salutation "Sir" or "Dear Sir" and phrases such as "We extend an invitation to His Royal Highness to open our new sports complex. It would give great pleasure to us and all sportsmen and sportswomen in our area should Prince Philip agree to honour our Society in this way".

An invitation to Her Majesty Queen Elizabeth The Queen Mother

The invitation should be addressed to—

> The Private Secretary to H.M. Queen Elizabeth The Queen Mother,
> Clarence House,
> St. James's,
> LONDON, S.W.1.

commencing the letter with "Sir" or "Dear Sir" and incorporating phrases such as, "convey an invitation to Her Majesty to perform the opening of our Training Centre. We very much hope that Queen Elizabeth The Queen Mother will graciously agree to honour our Society on this important occasion".

111

Invitations to other members of the Royal Family should be addressed to their households as follows and it should be noted that the sons and daughters of a Sovereign are styled "The" before Prince or Princess, e.g. H.R.H. The Prince of Wales; H.R.H. The Duke of York; H.R.H. The Prince Edward; H.R.H. The Princess Royal; H.R.H. The Princess Margaret.

The Prince and Princess of Wales

Letters should be sent to—

> The Private Secretary to The Prince and Princess of Wales,
> Buckingham Palace,
> LONDON, S.W.1.

The Duke and Duchess of York

> The Private Secretary to H.R.H. The Duke of York,
> Buckingham Palace,
> LONDON, S.W.1.

H.R.H. The Prince Edward

> The Private Secretary to H.R.H. The Prince Edward,
> Buckingham Palace,
> LONDON, S.W.1.

H.R.H. The Princess Royal

The Private Secretary to H.R.H. The Princess
Royal,
Buckingham Palace,
LONDON, S.W.1

H.R.H. The Princess Margaret, Countess of Snowdon

The Private Secretary to H.R.H. The Princess
Margaret,
Kensington Palace,
LONDON, W.8.

The Duke and Duchess of Gloucester

The Private Secretary to H.R.H. The Duke of
Gloucester,
Kensington Palace,
LONDON, W.8.

H.R.H. Princess Alice, Duchess of Gloucester

The Private Secretary to H.R.H. Princess
Alice, Duchess of Gloucester,
Kensington Palace,
LONDON, W.8.

The Duke and Duchess of Kent

The Private Secretary to H.R.H. The Duke of
Kent,
York House,
St. James's Palace,
LONDON, S.W.1.

113

H.R.H. Princess Alexandra, The Hon. Mrs. Angus Ogilvy

> The Lady-in-Waiting to H.R.H. Princess Alexandra,
> 22 Friary Court,
> St James's Palace,
> LONDON, S.W.1.

The salutation in this case should be "Madam" or "Dear Madam".

If extending an invitation to one of a pair, e.g. The Duchess of Kent, the initial invitation should be addressed as above, i.e. The Private Secretary to H.R.H. The Duke of Kent.

When dealing with correspondence issuing from replies received from the Royal Households, letters should be addressed to the person who has signed the reply. Should you be unaware of the correct style and designation of the writer, this can be found in the current issue of Whitaker's Almanack, under the heading The Queen's Household or Royal Households.

4. ROYAL VISITS

The tendency these days is for the more informal Royal visit, this wish often being expressed by members of the Royal family when agreeing to accept engagements. Even so there are certain rules of conduct which must be observed.

(a) For a Civic Occasion

If the Royal visit is a civic occasion, then the Lord Lieutenant will, prior to the visit, have worked out a detailed timetable and plan, which in turn will have been approved by the Royal household. On such an occasion the Lord Lieutenant will receive the Royal visitor on arrival and will introduce the Civic Head, who in turn will present those who are to have the honour of meeting the Royal Visitor.

The manner of presentation to the Royal Visitor should be made by the Civic Head as informally as possible, in some such words as, "May I present to Your Majesty, my wife, who is my Mayoress", or, "May I present our Deputy Mayor, Councillor John Blank, Ma'am".

It is usual for those to be presented to be assembled in a line and as the Royal Visitor passes down the line, the Civic Head walks on the left of the Royal Visitor announcing the names of those being presented.

If the occasion is graced by the presence of a Royal couple, as for example, The Queen accompanied by the Duke of Edinburgh, or the Prince of Wales accompanied by the Princess of Wales, then the Civic Head's lady or escort accompanies the Prince Phillip or Princess Diana, as the case may be.

If the Royal Visitor takes part in a procession, the Mayor or civic leader should either precede the Royal Visitor or walk on the left.

(b) For a Non-Civic Occasion

For a non-civic occasion, such as Princess Alice, Duchess of Gloucester, visiting Branches of the W.R.V.S. when the Civic Head has been invited to be present to receive Her Royal Highness, the correct procedure would be for the civic leader to await the arrival of the Royal car and welcome the Royal visitor as she alights. After presenting his lady, if she is present, the civic leader should then escort Her Royal Highness to the W.R.V.S. members and workers. As the Royal visitor is about to depart, the civic leader should step forward and escort Her Royal Highness to the waiting car.

5. ATTENDANCE AT A ROYAL GARDEN PARTY

The object of the Royal Garden Parties is to enable Her Majesty to entertain large numbers of people from all walks of life and from all parts of the United Kingdom and the Commonwealth, and in turn this gives the guests an opportunity of visiting Buckingham Palace and seeing something of the interior of the Palace as well as the grounds.

In order to achieve this end, the Lord Chamberlain allocates a number of invitations to various public bodies, such as charitable organisations, the hospital service, the civil service and local government. These bodies, in turn, decide which of their members are to be honoured by receiving an invitation.

In certain instances, a man and wife may be allowed to take unmarried daughters over eighteen years of age.

The gold embossed invitation card bearing the Royal Crest states that the party will be from 4 p.m. to 6 p.m. although all the gates to the Palace open at 3.15 p.m. Full details regarding the approaches to the Palace and parking facilities are sent along with the invitation, together with a car parking label.

After passing through the Palace forecourt and the main entrance into the forty-acre garden, choose a table at which to take tea and occupy the chairs. Immediately tea starts to be served from the main marquee one of the party should collect refreshments. On hearing the National Anthem played by the military bands one can assume that the Queen and other members of the Royal family have joined their guests in the garden.

The Lord Chamberlain and gentlemen ushers escort Her Majesty and other members of the Royal Family as they stroll among groups of guests on their way to the Royal marquee.

Guests should make a point of seeing the following—

1. The Royal marquee (easily distinguished by its red and gold canopy) where the formal presentations take place.

2. The Diplomatic Corps marquee.

3. The play-house on the outskirts of the garden.

117

On returning through the Palace galleries be sure to see the displays of china in the wall cabinets and on leaving if you wish to record your visit in Her Majesty's Visitors' Book go to the Police Box just inside the North Centre Gate, i.e. the one on the right hand side when looking at the front of the building, where you will be given the opportunity of signing the Palace Visitors' Book.

Garden Party invitations state "Morning Dress, Uniform or Lounge Suit". In recent years as the invitations tend to spread over an ever-widening and more varied strata of society, more and more dark lounge suits appear, although this is one of the few occasions when a man not owning morning dress, can hire for a reasonable fee, a superbly tailored morning coat, striped trousers and grey top hat to make him feel really good and to make the occasion a never-to-be forgotten one.

Women wear afternoon dress with hats and gloves, unless representing a uniformed group, in which event full dress uniform is correct wear.

Civic leaders may wear their badge of office on a ribbon or pin, but under no circumstances must the chain be worn.

Cameras are not permitted inside the Palace so if you've spent the earth on your outfit and want a picture for the family album, be sure to make arrangements beforehand to have a photographer meet you outside the Palace Gates or by the Victoria monument.

6. ATTENDING AN INVESTITURE

The majority of persons whose names appear in the Honours Lists are invited to present themselves at Buckingham Palace for investiture by Her Majesty. On occasions when The Queen is ill or overseas, these Investitures are carried out by some other Member of the Royal Family.

A few recipients of awards, such as the Queen's Police Medal, are invested by the Lord Lieutenant of their particular County when he is visiting in the area.

Those invited to London are allowed to be accompanied by two guests of their own choosing who are able to see the whole ceremony.

Along with the summons to attend, come detailed instructions regarding time of arrival at the Palace and the method of entry. Once inside, the guests are ushered to their seats whilst those to be decorated have explained to them in full by a Member of the Royal Household, the entire procedure to be followed.

As at Royal Garden Parties, cameras are not allowed inside the Palace. If a photograph is desired it is advisable to make prior arrangements to meet a photographer outside the Palace.

7. TELEGRAMS OF CONGRATULATIONS FROM HER MAJESTY THE QUEEN

With the increasing longevity of life, more and more people are surviving to celebrate their diamond wedding anniversary, which marks 60 years of married life, and indeed, to live on to become centenarians. The highlight of such an occasion is the receipt of a telegram of congratulations from Her Majesty the Queen, but the arrangement for the notification of the event to the Palace often poses a problem for relatives.

By far the simplest way of dealing with this event is for the closest relative to obtain a copy of the marriage or birth certificate and call at the local Town Hall or Council Offices to see the Mayor's or Chairman's Secretary and request that the necessary details be forwarded to Buckingham Palace for the attention of the Private Secretary to Her Majesty.

The relative or other responsible person connected with the family could send the relevant details, together with a copy of the birth or marriage certificate directly to the Private Secretary to Her Majesty at Buckingham Palace.

This should be done at least four weeks prior to the celebration.

It is necessary for the Palace officials to have factual proof of the event and that is why it is advisable for the birth or marriage certificate or a certified copy to be sent to the Palace, along with the present address of those who are about to celebrate. The certificate will be returned by the Palace officials within a few days.

Should the original certificate have been mislaid or lost copies can be obtained either by calling or by writing to the Registrar of Births, Deaths and Marriages for the area where the birth or marriage was registered.

In the case of a birth certificate it will be helpful to supply the full name, date and place of birth with father's name and mother's maiden name, if known.

For a marriage certificate it will be helpful to find out the full name of the bride and groom, the date and place where the marriage took place.

If uncertain of the area where the event was originally registered application can be made by post to the General Register Office, St. Catherine's House, 10 Kingsway, WC2B 6JP if the event took place in England or Wales or if in Scotland to The Registrar General, New Register House, Edinburgh, Scotland, EH1 3YT, allowing at least three weeks for the return of the certificate.

In all cases there is a fee to cover the cost of providing the service, the current fees for a birth certificate being £5 for a full certificate or £2.50 for a short certificate from the local Registrar or £10 for a full certificate and £7.50 for a short copy by post from the Registrar-General. The fee for a copy of a marriage certificate is £5 if obtained locally or £10 by post from the Registrar-General. Cheques should be made payable to The Registrar-General. People living in the London area can, of course, make a personal visit to St. Catherine's House.

There have been many occasions where an elderly person has celebrated his or her birthday on a certain day throughout a long life, only to find when turning up their birth certificate that they have, in fact, a different birthday.

Because of the increasing incidence of Golden Weddings (fifty years) it is not possible for these to be acknowledged by a Royal greeting.

Chapter VII
PRECEDENCE

1. ORDER OF PRECEDENCE IN ENGLAND

The accepted Order of Precedence in England next after the Royal Family is as follows—

Archbishop of Canterbury.——

Lord High Chancellor.

Archbishop of York.

The Prime Minister.

Lord President of the Council.

Speaker of the House of Commons.

Lord Privy Seal.

High Commissioners of Commonwealth Countries and Ambassadors of Foreign States. ——

Dukes, according to their Patents of Creation.
- (1) Of England.
- (2) Of Scotland
- (3) Of Great Britain
- (4) Of Ireland
- (5) Those created since the Union.

Ministers and Envoys.

Eldest sons of Dukes of Blood Royal.

Marquesses, in same order as Dukes.

Dukes' eldest sons.

Earls, in same order as Dukes.

Younger sons of Dukes of Blood Royal.

Marquesses' eldest sons.

Dukes' younger sons.

Viscounts, in same order as Dukes.

Earls' eldest sons.

Marquesses' younger sons.

Bishop of London.

Bishop of Durham.

Bishop of Winchester.

All other English Bishops, according to their seniority of Consecration.

Secretaries of State, if of the degree of a Baron.

Barons, in same order as Dukes.

Treasurer of Her Majesty's Household.

Comptroller of Her Majesty's Household.

Vice-Chamberlain of Her Majesty's Household.

Secretaries of State under the degree of Baron.

Viscounts' eldest sons.

Earls' younger sons.

Barons' eldest sons.

Knights of the Garter if Commoners.

Privy Counsellors if of no higher rank.

Chancellor of the Exchequer.

Chancellor of the Duchy of Lancaster.

Lord Chief Justice of England.

Master of the Rolls.

President of the Family Division.

The Lords Justices of Appeal.

Judges of the High Court.

Vice-Chancellor of County Palatine of Lancaster.

Viscounts' younger sons.

Barons' younger sons.

Sons of Life Peers.

Baronets of either Kingdom (according to date of Patents).

Knights of the Thistle (if Commoners).

Knights Grand Cross of the Bath.

Members of the Order of Merit.

Knights Grand Commanders of the Star of India.

Knights Grand Cross of St. Michael and St. George.

Knights Grand Commanders of the Indian Empire.

Knights Grand Cross of the Royal Victorian Order.

Knights Grand Cross of Order of the British Empire.

Companions of Honour.

Knights Commanders of the above Orders.

Knights Bachelor.

Official Referees of The Supreme Court.

Circuit Judges and Judges of the Mayor's and City of London Court.

Companions and Commanders in following order—

Companions of the Bath.

Companions of the Star of India.

Companions of St. Michael and St. George.

Companions of the Indian Empire.

Commanders of the Royal Victorian Order.

Commanders of the British Empire.

Companions of the Distinguished Service Order.

Lieutenants of the Royal Victorian Order (4th class).

Officers of the Order of the British Empire.

Companions of the Imperial Service Order.

Eldest sons of younger sons of Peers.

Baronets' eldest sons.

Eldest sons of Knights in same order as their Fathers.

Members of the Royal Victorian Order (5th class).

Members of the Order of the British Empire.

Younger sons of the younger sons of Peers.

Baronets' younger sons.

Younger sons of Knights in the same order as their Fathers.

Naval, Military and Air, and other Esquires by Office.

Women

Women take the same rank as their husbands or as their eldest brothers, but the daughter of a Peer who marries a Commoner retains her title as Lady or Honourable, as in the case of the late Lady Dorothy MacMillan, who as Lady Dorothy Cavendish daughter of the Duke of Devonshire, married Mr Harold MacMillan but retained her title as Lady.

2. PRECEDENCE IN SCOTLAND is quite different from that in England and follows the following order after the Royal family—

Lords Lieutenant of Counties.

Lord Provosts of Counties of Cities, and Sheriffs Principal.

Lord Chancellor of Great Britain.

Moderator of the Assembly of the Church of Scotland.

The Prime Minister.

Keepers of the Great Seal and of the Privy Seal.

Hereditary Lord High Constable of Scotland.

Hereditary Master of the Household.

Dukes (successively) of England, Scotland, Great Britain and United Kingdom (including Ireland since date of Union).

Eldest sons of Royal Dukes.

Marquesses, in same order as Dukes.

Dukes' eldest sons.

Earls, in same order as Dukes.

Younger sons of Dukes of Blood Royal.

Marquesses' elder sons.

Dukes' younger sons.

Keepers of the Great Seal and of the Privy Seal (successively if not Peers).

Lord Justice General.

Lord Clerk Register.

Lord Advocate.

Lord Justice Clerk.

Viscounts, in same order as Dukes.

Earls' eldest sons.

Marquesses' younger sons.

Lord Barons, in same order as Dukes.

Viscounts' eldest sons.

Earls' younger sons.

Lord Barons' eldest sons.

Knights of the Garter.

Privy Counsellors not included in any of the above ranks.

Senators of College of Justice (known as Lords of Session).

Viscounts' younger sons.

Lord Barons' younger sons.

Sons of Life Peers.

Baronets.

Knights of the Thistle.

Knights of other Orders as in England.

Solicitor General for Scotland.

Lord Lyon King of Arms.

Sheriffs Principal (except when in their own locality).

Knights Bachelor.

Sheriffs Substitute.

Companions of Orders as in England.

Commanders of Royal Victorian and British Empire Orders.

Eldest sons of younger sons of Peers.

Companions of Distinguished Service Order.

Lieutenants of the Royal Victorian Order (4th Class).

Officers of the British Empire Order.

Baronets' eldest sons.

Knights' eldest sons successively.

Members of the the Royal Victorian Order (5th Class).

Members of the British Empire Order.

Baronets' younger sons.

Knights' younger sons.

Queen's Counsel.

Esquires.

3. LOCAL PRECEDENCE

Many charitable and social organisations invite the Lord Mayor, Mayor or Chairman of their Council, along with his or her partner, to attend their annual meeting, dinner or other social function and on these occasions, as indeed on all occasions when a civic head is present, it is essential that he or she be accorded the precedence due to the office. This is part of the general law of our country and is contained in Section 3(4) of The Local Government Act 1972, which says that the chairman of a district council will have precedence in the district, whether as mayor, in the case of a district which has obtained a charter conferring borough status, or as chairman of the district council where no such charter has been granted.

Unless the Lord Mayor, Mayor or Chairman occupies the chair at a gathering, he should be seated on the immediate right of the chairman of the meeting and if asked to speak on a toast list, organisers should accord the civic head the privilege of being the first to propose or respond to the toast which immediately follows the Loyal Toast.

The Lord Mayor, Mayor or Chairman should always be seated on the platform or at the top table. When the Mayoress attends a function alone, similar arrangements should be made for her.

When the Deputy Lord Mayor, Deputy Mayor or Vice-Chairman of the Council is present, arrangements similar to these should be made for his or her convenience and when such a dignitary is attending a function in place of the Lord Mayor, Mayor or Chairman, he or she should be accorded the full precedence of the Lord Mayor, Mayor or Chairman.

Some of the smaller boroughs which existed prior to 1974 are no longer entitled to borough status although they retain their councils at parish level as "successor parishes". The 1972 Act gave these parish councils the right to pass a resolution, by a simple majority of those members of the council present and voting, to adopt the status of "town', for the area of the parish and the style of "town council" for the authority. Furthermore, the chairman and vice-chairman of the council are entitled to be known as the town mayor and deputy town mayor respectively.

When acting in the area of the town, the town mayor should be accorded the courtesy of precedence as a civic head, providing the mayor of the new district or borough is not present, in which case the charter mayor or chairman is the person who takes precedence.

Precedence for other local officers of dignity, which can include sheriffs of cities and towns, high stewards, and honorary recorders as well as honorary freemen, is a matter of local custom and organisations wishing to entertain any of these civic personalities would do well to seek the guidance of the secretary to the civic head as to local procedure.

In somewhat lighter vein it is interesting to note that in her autobiography, "Sing As We Go", the late Dame Gracie Fields, D.B.E., recalled that even when twenty-nine years of age and topping the bills in show business in London she considered there were four beings of tremendous importance: God, the King and Queen and the Mayor of Rochdale, her home town in that order. When Sir Gerald du Maurier, who was then London's most successful actor-manager called on her to offer her a lead in one of his productions, never having met a Knight of the Realm before, she reckoned he must be even more important than the Mayor!

Chapter VIII
REGALIA, INSIGNIA AND DECORATIONS

1. DEFINITION

The word "regalia" denotes the emblems of sovereignty. They consist of the crowns, sceptre, orb and other priceless articles used at a coronation. "Insignia" is the word to describe signs of office and honours held by the wearers. A new Life Peer will be seen in a television news bulletin or pictured in the newspaper wearing his or her Peer's robe when introduced in the House of Lords. We see pictures of Judges wearing their gowns and wigs; we see our clergy wearing their clerical collars; our Lord Mayors and Mayors wearing the civic robes and chains on some ceremonial occasion in the civic calendar and almost every edition of a local weekly newspaper carries a picture the the President of the local Soroptimist Club wearing a badge on a ribbon, presiding at some fund raising event. All are seen wearing the "insignia" of their office.

When attending in State to open a new session of Parliament, Her Majesty the Queen wears a Crown which is part of the Royal "regalia". At the annual meeting of a local authority when a new Mayor is elected, almost all persons taking office will wear the civic robe and chain, these being part of the "insignia" of the office.

2. ORDERS, DECORATIONS AND MEDALS

At least twice a year, on the occasion of The Queen's Official Birthday in June and to mark the commencement of the New Year, the Honours Lists publish the names of men and women from all walks of life in Britain and the Commonwealth who have rendered what is regarded as distinguished service in their particular sphere of activity. The recognition of their services range over a wide variety of Orders of Chivalry, decorations and medals with each award having its own specific insignia, some in the form of a star, some as crosses and some as medals but all are most attractive jewels.

When invested with their award, each recipient receives from the Lord Chamberlain's Office a booklet compiled by The Central Chancery of the Order of Knighthoods giving precise advice on when and how to wear the insignia of the award.

The rules state that members of the various Orders of Chivalry and all persons who have been awarded decorations and medals, may should they wish to do so, wear their insignia on those occasions when the person responsible for organising a function deems it fitting for decorations to be worn. On such occasions it would also be appropriate to wear any military campaign stars and medals to which the holder may be entitled. The occasions are divided into two categories—

(i)   When The Queen, The Queen Mother or a Member of the Royal Family who is a Royal

133

Highness is present. The host should ascertain from the appropriate Royal Household whether it is desired that decorations should be worn and this should be indicated on the invitation.

(ii) On all other occasions the host should decide whether the nature or importance of the occasion makes it appropriate for decorations to be worn and then issue instructions on the invitation. Even so, on all such occasions the wearing of insignia will be at the discretion of the holder.

(a) Orders of Chivalry

The first three of the British Orders of Chivalry are the exclusive Order of the Garter, Order of the Thistle and Order of St. Patrick.

Other Orders of Chivalry are divided into several classes, the first two of which carry a Knighthood for a man and where women are eligible for the Order they are created Dames. Some of the Orders also have a civil and a military division.

Below are the Orders with the appropriate letters after names for class one and two:—

	Knight (or Dame) Grand Cross	Knight Commander	Dame Commander
Order of the Bath	G.C.B.	K.C.B.	D.C.B.
Order of the Star of India	G.C.S.I.	K.C.S.I.	
Order of St. Michael and St. George	G.C.M.G.	K.C.M.G.	D.C.M.G.

Order of the Indian Empire	G.C.I.E.	K.C.I.E.	
Royal Victorian Order	G.C.V.O.	K.C.V.O.	D.C.V.O.
Order of the British Empire	G.B.E.	K.B.E.	D.B.E.

All those honoured by the above awards are addressed as "Sir" or "Dame", *e.g.* Miss Kiri Te Kanawa became Dame Kiri Te Kanawa, D.B.E., when she was made a Dame Commander of The Most Excellent Order of the British Empire.

Should a person already in possession of a higher title receive an award, then the appropriate letters of the lower award are appended to the name, an example of this being when The Countess of Brecknock was created a Dame Commander of the Order of the British Empire she became The Countess of Brecknock, D.B.E.

Honorary Knighthoods

Non-British subjects can, by a personal gift from Her Majesty be awarded Honorary Knighthoods of the British Empire, two recent appointments being Bob Geldof, K.B.E., and J. P. Getty II, K.B.E. Both remain "Mister" but should either of these gentlemen adopt British citizenship in the future they will become Sir Bob or Sir John Paul. An instance of this occured in 1985 when the now Sir Yehudi Menuhin, O.M., applied for and was granted British citizenship. Sir Yehudi was born in New York of Russian Jewish parents and was an American citizen although his music is known and heard worldwide. In recognition of his great contribution to music and in particular for his work in founding the Yehudi Menuhin School of

135

Music at Stoke d'Abernon, Surrey, The Queen appointed him an Honorary Knight in 1965. Twenty years later in 1985 when the Honorary Knight became a British citizen he became Sir Yehudi Menuhin, and was more recently honoured by Her Majesty by being appointed to The Order of Merit.

The following list shows the order in which Orders, decorations and medals should be worn in the United Kingdom, certain countries of the Commonwealth and in the Overseas Territories, with the letters which can be placed after names,

Victoria Cross	This honour precedes all others irrespective of date of award.
George Cross	G.C. After V.C. this honour precedes all others.
Order of the Garter	K.G.
Order of the Thistle	K.T.
Order of St. Patrick	K.P.
Order of the Bath	G.C.B., K.C.B., or D.C.B. (see p. 134)
Order of Merit	O.M.
Order of the Star of India	G.C.S.I or K.C.S.I (see p. 134)

Order of St. Michael and St. George	G.C.M.G., K.C.M.G. or D.C.M.G. (see p. 134)
Order of the Indian Empire	G.C.I.E. or K.C.I.E. (see p. 135)
Order of the Crown of India	K.C.I.E.
Royal Victorian Order	G.C.V.O., K.C.V.O. or D.C.V.O. (see p. 135)
Order of the British Empire	G.B.E., K.B.E. or D.B.E. (see p. 135)
Order of the Companions of Honour	C.H.
Companion of the Order of the Bath	C.B.
Companion of the Order of the Star of India	C.S.I.
Companion of the Order of St. Michael and St. George	C.M.G.
Companion of the Order of the Indian Empire	C.I.E.
Commander of the Royal Victorian Order	C.V.O.
Commander of the Order of the British Empire	C.B.E.
Distinguished Service Order	D.S.O.

Lieutenant of the Royal Victorian Order (Class 4)	L.V.O.
Order of the British Empire (Class IV)	O.B.E.
Imperial Service Order	I.S.O.
Member of the Royal Victorian Order (Class 5)	M.V.O.
Member of the Order of the British Empire	M.B.E.
Baronet's Badge	Bart. or Bt.
Knight Bachelor's Badge	
Indian Order of Merit (Military)	I.O.M.

(b) Decorations

Royal Red Cross (Class I)	R.R.C.
Distinguised Service Cross	D.S.C.
Military Cross	M.C.
Distinguished Flying Cross	D.F.C.
Air Force Cross	A.F.C.
Royal Red Cross (Class II)	A.R.R.C.
Order of British India	O.B.I.
Kaisar-i-Hind Medal.	
Order of St. John.	

(c) Medals for Gallantry and Distinguished Conduct

Distinguished Conduct Medal	D.C.M.

Conspicuous Gallantry Medal	C.G.M.
George Medal	G.M.
Queen's Police Medal for Gallantry	Q.P.M.G.
Queen's Fire Service Medal for Gallantry	Q.F.S.M.G.
Royal West African Frontier Force Distinguished Conduct Medal	D.C.M.
King's African Rifles Distinguished Conduct Medal	D.C.M.
Indian Distinguished Service Medal	D.S.M.
Military Medal	M.M.
Distinguished Flying Medal	D.F.M.
Air Force Medal	A.F.M.
Medal for Saving Life at Sea	S.G.M.
Indian Order of Merit (Civil)	I.O.M.
Queen's Gallantry Medal	Q.G.M.
Royal Victorian Medal	R.V.M.
British Empire Medal	B.E.M.
Canada Medal	C.M.
Queen's Police Medal for Distinguished Service	Q.P.M.
Queen's Fire Service Medal for Distinguished Service	Q.F.S.M.
War medals, in order of date	

of campaign for which
awarded.
Polar Medals.
Jubilee, Coronation and
Durbar Medals, in order of
date awarded.
Efficiency and Long Service
Decorations and Medals.

(d) War Campaign Medals and Stars

Medals and stars awarded for service during the
first world war 1914-1919 should be worn in the following order—1914 Star, 1914-1915 Star, British
War Medal, Mercantile Marine War Medal, Victory
Medal, Territorial Force War Medal, India General
Service Medal (1908) for operations in Afghanistan
1919.

Campaign medals and stars awarded for service in
the second world war 1939-1945 should be worn in
the following order—1939-1945 Star, Atlantic Star,
Air Crew Europe Star, Africa Star, Pacific Star, Italy
Star, France and Germany Star, Defence Medal,
Volunteer Service Medal of Canada, War Medal
1939-1945, Africa Service Medal for the Union of
South Africa, India Service Medal, New Zealand War
Service Medal, Southern Rhodesia Service Medal,
Australia Service Medal.

(e) Mention in Despatches

The Emblem of bronze oak leaves denotes a Mention in Despatches during the first world war 1914-

1919 and should be worn on the ribbon of the Victory Medal.

The single bronze oak leaf Emblem, signifying in the armed forces and the Merchant Navy, either a Mention in Despatches, a King's Commendation for brave conduct, or a King's Commendation for valuable service in the air, if granted for service in the second world war, 1939-1945, is worn on the ribbon of the War Medal 1939-1945. If the War Medal has not been granted, the Emblem is worn directly on the coat, after any Medal ribands.

Mention in Despaches 1945 and subsequently is a single bronze oak leaf Emblem and if granted for service in operations after the cessation of the second world war, is worn on the riband of the appropriate General Service or Campaign Medal. If such a medal has not been granted, the Emblem is worn directly on the coat after any medal ribands.

The single bronze oak leaf Emblem is also used in the Forces to denote a King's or Queen's Commendation for brave conduct or a King's or Queen's Commendation for valuable service in the air granted since the cessation of hostilities in the second world war.

The Emblem of silver laurel leaves granted to civilians, other than those in the Merchant Navy, denotes a King's Commendation for brave conduct during the second world war, 1939-1945 and is worn on the riband of the Defence Medal. When the Defence Medal has not been granted or the award is for services subsequent to the war, the Emblem of silver laurel leaves is worn directly on the coat after any Medal ribands.

The oval silver Badge granted to denote a civil King's Commendation or Queen's Commendation for valuable service in the air is worn on the coat immediately below any Medals or Medal ribands, or on civil air line uniform, is worn on the panel of the left breast pocket.

Collectors, historians and others interested in having more information on this subject should consult Ribbons and Medals by the late Captain H. Taprell Dorling, D.S.O., R.N. (Taffrail), in association with L. F. Guille, published by George Philip and Son Ltd., 12 Long Acre, London W.C.2. This has long been recognised as being the standard reference work on this subject.

3. MINIATURES

Some but not all the insignia of peace time Crown honours can be worn as miniatures at evening functions, along with miniatures of military campaign medals and stars.

The miniatures can be obtained from most good jewellers in the provinces or direct from—

> Spink and Son Limited, 5 King Street, London, S.W.1.
>
> or
>
> Garrard and Company Limited, 112 Regent Street, London, W.1.

4. WEARING OF ORDERS, DECORATIONS, MINIATURES AND MEDALS WITH FULL EVENING DRESS AND DINNER JACKET

The following are the occasions when Orders, decorations, miniatures and medals would be worn with full evening dress, on the advice of the Lord Chamberlain's Office:—

1. At all parties and dinners attended by The Queen, The Queen Mother or a Member of The Royal Family who is a Royal Highness, the host or hostess having ascertained from the Royal Household whether it is desired that decorations should be worn.

2. At all Parties and Dinners given in houses of Ambassadors, High Commissioners and Ministers accredited to St. James's Palace, unless otherwise notified by the Ambassador, High Commissioner or Minister concerned.

3. At all Official Dinners and Receptions, including Naval, Military and Air Force Dinners, Dinners of City Livery Companies, and Public Dinners. (The word "Decorations" on the invitation card is an intimation from the host that the entertainment is an official one.)

4. On official occasions when entertained by such people as—

   Her Majesty's Lieutenant of the County within his County.

> The High Sheriff of a County within his County.
>
> Lord Mayors and Mayors.
>
> Lord Provosts and Provosts.

Miniature decorations and medals should be worn when attending a function for which the invitation states, "Dinner Jacket—Decorations".

5. WEARING ORDERS, DECORATIONS AND MEDALS WITH DAY DRESS

Full size decorations and medals mounted on a medal bar are worn with Lounge Suits at Remembrance Sunday Services, Royal British Legion gatherings and Service occasions. At some evening functions it may be more appropriate to wear miniatures.

Only those full-size Orders, decorations and medals normally mounted on a medal bar should be worn on an overcoat.

A civic head may wear full-size decorations and medals on the left hand side of a civic robe, along with any military campaign medals and stars which he or she is entitled to wear.

6. RIBBONS

The Lord Chamberlain has stated that the ribbons of the Orders, decorations and medals may be worn on all occasions at the discretion of the holder, for example, a member of H.M. Forces, a Policeman, a

Commissionaire or any person wearing uniform, can, at his or her discretion, wear the ribbons of any Orders, decorations or medals they have been awarded.

The method of wearing the ribbons, which is the same in all cases, both for men and women, is as follows—

A piece of the ribbon, one and a half inches wide, or the width of the medal ribbon, and half an inch in depth, mounted on a bar of metal in the form of a brooch, is worn on the left breast of the coat, or in a corresponding place on the dress, as the case may be.

7. FOREIGN ORDERS, DECORATIONS AND MEDALS

War-time resistance and the uneasy times in which we live have been responsible for many United Kingdom private persons being decorated by foreign countries. One such was Mrs. Odette Hallowes, G.C., M.B.E., who as Odette Churchill was awarded the Legion d'Honneur for her part as a British agent in the French underground movement during the last war.

The Lord Chamberlain's Office advise that it is The Queen's wish that Her Majesty's subjects should not accept and wear foreign awards without permission and if such permission does not accompany the foreign award then application should be made to The Secretary of State for Foreign and Commonwealth

145

Affairs, at the Foreign and Commonwealth Office, Downing Street, SW1A 2AL.

Permission, if granted will be either restricted to allowing the insignia to be worn only on particular occasions associated with the country concerned, or for unrestricted wearing of the insignia on any occasion. Foreign medals may be mounted permanently on a medal bar (full-size and miniature).

8. HERALDRY

Heraldry is the general term denoting the business of heralds and armorial bearings. During the Crusades in the Middle Ages, the Knights assumed personal devices as distinguishing signs in the field and the practice of embroidering the personal devices of a Knight on the surcoat over the armour originated the term "Coat of Arms". After the Crusades they came to appear on personal apparel, books, seals, signet rings, windows, furniture and tapestry hangings.

Arms are granted in England by the College of Arms which was formed in 1483 by Richard III and in Scotland by the Lord Lyon King-at-Arms. Broadly speaking those eligible for the Grant of Arms, apart from individuals, include the holders of certain offices such as Bishops, public bodies, Corporations, schools and bodies incorporated by Act of Parliament, or Royal Charter, and in certain instances business houses.

The College of Arms has published a series of leaflets dealing with the work of the College and requests for copies of the leaflets, or for advice on any point in connection with the granting of arms should be sent directly to the College of Arms, Queen Victoria Street, London, EC4V 4BT.

An example of a full achievement of Arms would contain a Shield decorated with heraldic figures or "charges" and such accessories as a Crest fixed to a military Helm, Supporters and Mantling and Wreath with a Compartment leading to a Scroll containing a Motto. All these heraldic technical terms have precise meanings and those who would like to learn more about it would be well rewarded by reading "Simple Heraldry Cheerfully Illustrated", by Iain Moncreiffe and Don Pottinger, published by Nelson, and other more detailed works mentioned in the list of useful books in Appendix D at page 215.

9. CIVIC INSIGNIA

(a) The Mayoral Robe and Chain

The general rules accepted by most authorities for wearing of civic insignia are set out in "Civic Ceremonial" by G. N. Waldram, M.V.O., published by Shaw and Sons Ltd., although the wearing of mayoral robes and chain and badge of office depends on local custom to a large extent.

A civic leader should not wear his robe outside his own borough unless invited to do so by the mayor of the other authority. This rule applies also to the wear-

147

ing of the chain or badge of office. If visiting outside his own borough and wishing to wear his chain or badge, the correct procedure is to first obtain permission from the leader of the Borough to be visited.

The mayoral chain and badge should never be worn with the uniform of any of the Armed Services, but may be worn with the uniform of the Lieutenancy of the County. Mayors who are clergy may wear the chain or badge with their clerical dress.

There are certain civic occasions, amongst them the annual meeting of the Council and Civic Sunday, when the wearing of the mayoral robe and chain, with the mace carried in procession, symbolise for all to see, our proud heritage and tradition of democratic government and add immeasurably to the dignity and grace of the occasion.

The late Sir Mortimer Wheeler, in his book "Still Digging", wrote—"It so happens that I have had a long experience of mayors and am amongst their most fervent admirers. They represent the head of England, these proud, courteous, friendly, sensible folk, who rise from their railway ticket offices and their shops to attend in state to the affairs of their fellow citizens".

(b) The Ex-mayor

Many authorities make a practice of presenting badges to retiring mayors and ex-mayoresses. Its form varies; sometimes it is fashioned to be worn round the neck or on the lapel of a coat and one north-country town has adopted the novel idea of incorporating an enamelled emblem of the coat of arms mounted in a ring for its ex-mayoresses.

These symbols of past office are only applicable to be worn within the civic area to which they are associated. It cannot be held that a past Mayor's badge is a decoration for wearing on general occasions.

10. BADGES OF OFFICE

Many organisations such as the Chambers of Commerce and Trade, Rotary Clubs, Round Tables, Inner Wheel Clubs, Business and Professional Women's Clubs, Soroptimists, etc., provide a badge of office for their President to wear at their own gatherings and when representing their organisation at other public functions.

It is appropriate for these badges to be worn on all occasions when an invitation clearly states that the person invited is invited as "President of the ...." and the word "Decorations" appears on the invitation.

11. EMBLEMS AND LOGOTYPES

Few organisations exist for long before it is suggested that they adopt an emblem or logotype for use on their notepaper, blazer pockets and membership cards, etc. These emblems, not designed according to the strict rules of blazonry laid down by the

College of Arms, are termed Badges and can be used at will by the governing body of the organisation, providing that no part of the badge is copied from any existing Arms.

Local Authorities are frequently asked for permission to allow their Arms or part of the Arms to be used by local organisations such as football clubs, swimming clubs, etc., within their area. As has been stated earlier, the right to a Coat of Arms is conferred by a grant of Arms made under royal authority and it is a limited right and not one which can be passed on to a third party. Here it must be pointed out that there is a relevant legal point which draws an important distinction between the use of the display of arms. "Use" means using them as if they were one's own—which, if they are not, is usurpation. But one can display the arms quite blamelessly if they bear an inscription which clearly shows whose they are. Under this heading perhaps come those souvenir teaspoons decorated with the local Coat of Arms, with the name of the authority shewn under the crest.

12. FLYING THE FLAG

There are established rules for the flying of the Union Flag on government buildings and these are set out in full each year in Whitaker's Almanack. Almost all local authorities and major business concerns throughout the country observe these rules and fly their flags from their headquarter buildings.

150

Many of our Councils have their own flag featuring their Coat of Arms or civic emblem and this will be flown from the civic headquarters on such occasions as—

The Annual Meeting of the Council and Election of Lord Mayor/Mayor/Chairman,
Civic Sunday,
Civic Receptions.

Some local authorities have made a practice of observing national Saints days by flying the St. George's Cross on St. George's Day, 23rd April; the Welsh flag with the red dragon on a green and white field on St. David's Day, 1st March and the cross of St. Andrew on St. Andrew's Day, 30th November, in addition to the United Nations Flag on United Nations Day, 24th October.

Leading industrial concerns, having their own Company flag, make a practice of flying it from the flagmast on important days in the affairs of their Company, such as the signing of an important new contract and the presentation of The Queen's Award for Export Achievement or The Queen's Award for Technological Achievement.

It has become the practice for many community organisations who have their own Centre or Clubroom to have a flagpole and their own flag, sometimes the Union Flag or sometimes a flag bearing their emblem or the name of their organisation and one of their number will take it upon himself or herself to hoist the flag on appropriate occasions to record national or local events.

It would give more significance to the flying of the flag if a small neatly written or typewritten notice were to be placed on a board attached to the flagpole stating why the flag is flying. Some such wording as, "The flag is flying in celebration of the Silver Jubilee of our Guild", or "The flag is flying at half mast as a mark of respect for .... formerly a member", would let the general public know why the flag is flying.

13. FLAGS ON CARS

Where small flags are flown on official cars, care should be taken to make sure that there is no danger of the flag causing any obstruction of vision to the driver, particularly at night.

Appendix A
SPECIMEN SPEECHES

(a) Proposing a toast to The British Red Cross Society.

MR. CHAIRMAN, MR. WOOD, LADIES AND GENTLEMEN,

1. **IT GIVES ME PLEASURE** TO PROPOSE THE TOAST TO THE BRITISH RED CROSS SOCIETY ... AND IN DOING SO I WELCOME THIS OPPORTUNITY OF EXPRESSING THANKS ON BEHALF OF OUR TOWN TO OUR LOCAL DIVISION ... NOT ONLY FOR THEIR KIND HOSPITALITY TO US THIS EVENING ... BUT IN A WIDER SENSE I AM GLAD TO PAY MY TRIBUTE TO YOUR SPLENDID ORGANISATION FOR ALL THE EXCELLENT WORK YOU CARRY OUT ... MOST OF IT IN A VOLUNTARY CAPACITY.

2. **HISTORY ACCORDS** A RIGHTFUL PLACE TO MEN OF VISION ... AS INDEED IT HAS TO HENRY DUNANT ... THE MAN RESPONSIBLE FOR THE FORMATION OF THE INTERNATIONAL COMMITTEE OF THE RED CROSS ... FROM WHICH SPRINGS THE BRITISH RED CROSS SOCIETY AND OUR LOCAL DIVISION OF THE ORGANISATION.

153

3. **MY WAR TIME EXPERIENCES** IN MANY THEATRES OF THE WAR ... LEFT ME IN NO DOUBT AS TO THE VALUE OF YOUR SOCIETY IN WAR TIME ... BUT IN PEACE TIME WHEN NATURAL DISASTERS OCCUR ... WE HAVE GROWN ACCUSTOMED TO LOOK TO YOUR MEMBERS FOR HELP AND COMFORT ... AND NEVER HAVE YOU BEEN FOUND WANTING. EARTHQUAKE ... FLOOD ... AND FAMINE DISASTERS IN OTHER LANDS ... TO THE LESS SPECTACULAR JOB OF GIVING FIRST AID ON FOOTBALL GROUNDS OR IN PUBLIC PLACES ... WE KNOW WE CAN RELY ON YOUR MEMBERS ... SENIORS AND CADETS ALIKE ... AND ON BEHALF OF THE PUBLIC AT LARGE ... I SAY A HEARTFELT THANK YOU FOR ALL YOU HAVE DONE AND CONTINUE TO DO.

4. **I WOULD LIKE TO CONCLUDE** BY QUOTING TO YOU THE WORDS FLORENCE NIGHTINGALE WROTE TO YOUR FOUNDER ... "IT IS A WORK TRULY OF GOD AND OF GOD'S CIVILISATION".

5. **LADIES AND GENTLEMEN** ... I HAVE PLEASURE IN ASKING YOU TO STAND WITH ME AND DRINK TO THE BRITISH RED CROSS SOCIETY, COUPLED WITH THE NAME OF THE REGIONAL OFFICER ... MR. WOOD ...

(b) Proposing a toast to The Industrial Life Offices.

MR. CHAIRMAN, MR. MAYOR, MADAM MAYORESS, LADIES AND GENTLEMEN,

1. **IT GIVES ME PLEASURE** TO HAVE THIS OPPORTUNITY OF PROPOSING THE TOAST TO "THE INDUSTRIAL LIFE OFFICES" AND IN SO DOING WOULD LIKE TO COMPLIMENT AND THANK THE VARIOUS INSURANCE COMPANIES AND THEIR OFFICERS WHO ARE OUR HOSTS TODAY ... FOR THE SPLENDOUR OF THEIR HOSPITALITY.

2. **IN MY ROLE** AS CHAIRMAN OF THE COUNCIL'S FINANCE AND ESTATES COMMITTEE ... I KNOW ONLY TOO WELL WHAT A TREMENDOUS PART OUR INSURANCE COMPANIES PLAY IN OUR NATIONAL ECONOMY ...

3. **THROUGH THE INVESTMENT** OF INSURANCE FUNDS COMES A CONSIDERABLE PART OF THE CAPITAL WHICH IS NEEDED TO KEEP THE NATIONAL ECONOMY FLEXIBLE TO MEET THE NEEDS OF INDUSTRY AND COMMERCE SEEKING CAPITAL RESOURCES ON COMPETITIVE TERMS ... WHEN I TELL YOU THAT ABOUT TWO FIFTHS OF BRITISH LIFE ASSURED FUNDS ARE INVESTED IN ORDINARY AND PREFERENCE SHARES AND DEBENTURES ... AND THAT THE BULK OF THE REMAINDER ARE DISTRIBUTED AMONG A WIDE RANGE OF GOVERNMENT SECURITIES ... MUNICIPAL LOANS ... PROPERTY AND MORTGAGES ... YOU WILL REALISE HOW VITAL IS THE CONTRIBUTION MADE BY OUR INSURANCE COMPANIES.

4. **IN MY OTHER ROLE** AS PRESIDENT OF OUR LOCAL NATIONAL SAVINGS COMMITTEE ... I AM WELL AWARE THAT ALTHOUGH WE HERE HAVE A SAVINGS RECORD OF WHICH WE ARE JUSTIFIABLY PROUD ... REGULAR THRIFT IS A HABIT WHICH DOES NOT COME EASY TO THE VAST MAJORITY OF PEOPLE ... AND THE WEEKLY OR MONTHLY VISIT OF THE "INSURANCE MAN" GOES A LONG WAY TO MAKE SURE THAT THE NEEDS OF THE FUTURE ARE NOT ALTOGETHER NEGLECTED ... I THINK IT IS LIKELY THAT IN MANY OF THE HOMES WHERE THE INSURANCE MAN MAKES HIS REGULAR CALLS ... THERE IS NO OTHER FORM OF REGULAR VOLUNTARY SAVING ... BECAUSE OF THIS THE ORDINARY FAMILIES OWE A DEBT OF GRATITUDE TO OUR INSURANCE COMPANIES FOR THE COMFORT WHICH A POLICY AFFORDS ON RETIREMENT ... OR IN TIMES OF BEREAVEMENT.

5. **SINCE THE INTRODUCTION** OF INDUSTRIAL LIFE ASSURANCE MORE THAN ONE HUNDRED AND TWENTY YEARS AGO BY A GROUP OF FAR SIGHTED PIONEERS ... THE PATTERN OF INSURANCE HAS CHANGED A GREAT DEAL ... GONE ARE THE PENNY POLICIES SO POPULAR WITH THE VICTORIAN WORKERS STRUGGLING TO SURVIVE ON MEAGRE PITTANCES ... IN THEIR PLACE HAS COME THE ENDOWMENT POLICY ... BUT STILL MEETING A NEED AS REAL TODAY AS IT WAS TO THE NINETEENTH CENTURY WORKER ... IN FACT, THE IDEA OF BEING ASSURED HAS BEEN WITH US FOR HUNDREDS OF YEARS ... DID NOT THE GREATEST OF ALL OUR ENGLISH BARDS WRITE AT THE TIME OF ELIZABETH THE FIRST ... AND

HERE I QUOTE SHAKESPEARE'S MACBETH ....
"BUT YET I'LL MAKE ASSURANCE DOUBLE SURE,
AND TAKE A BOND OF FATE, THAT I MAY TELL
PALE-HEARTED FEAR IT LIES, AND SLEEP IN SPITE
OF THUNDER."

6. **MR. CHAIRMAN,** THE INDUSTRIAL LIFE OFFICES
HAVE A RECORD OF WHICH YOU HAVE EVERY
REASON TO BE PROUD ... I WISH YOUR EFFORTS
EVERY SUCCESS IN THE FUTURE ... AND ASK YOU
... MR. MAYOR, MADAM MAYORESS, LADIES AND
GENTLEMEN, TO RISE AND DRINK WITH ME TO
"THE INDUSTRIAL LIFE OFFICES" ...

(c) Responding to a toast to The Local Authority at Annual Dinner of local Chamber of Trade and Commerce.

MR. PRESIDENT, LADIES AND GENTLEMEN,

1. **A LEADING POLITICIAN** IN THE THIRTIES ... ONCE REMARKED THAT HE HAD GROWN ACCUSTOMED IN HIS LONG YEARS AS A POLITICIAN ... NEVER TO BE ALLOWED TO ENJOY A DINNER WITHOUT HAVING TO MAKE A SPEECH IN RETURN ... NOW THAT I AM THE MAYOR OF OUR TOWN ... I AM FINDING THAT I TOO HAVE TO DO SOMETHING IN RETURN FOR MY DINNER ...

2. **FIRST OF ALL** ... MR. PRESIDENT, LADIES AND GENTLEMEN ... LET ME THANK YOUR LOCAL CHAMBER OF TRADE AND COMMERCE FOR THEIR KIND HOSPITALITY TO THE MAYORESS AND ME THIS EVENING ... WE ARE VERY PLEASED TO SHARE WITH YOU THIS IMPORTANT OCCASION IN YOUR YEAR FOR I CONSIDER YOUR ORGANISATION TO BE OF PARAMOUNT IMPORTANCE IN OUR COMMUNITY ... REPRESENTING AS IT DOES THE TRADE AND COMMERCE OF OUR TOWN ... AND OFFERING AS IT DOES FROM TIME TO TIME ADVICE AND SOMETIMES CRITICISM ... WHEN YOU THINK THE COUNCIL HAS MADE A FALSE DECISION.

3. **MY EXPERIENCE** HAS TAUGHT ME TO RESPECT ANY ORGANISATION WHICH OFFERS CONSTRUCTIVE CRITICISM AND HELPFUL SUGGESTIONS ...

IN FACT I WELCOME THEM ALWAYS ... FOR I REALISE THAT ANY ORGANISATION OFFERING CRITICISM OR SUGGESTIONS ... IS NOT A STAGNANT INDIFFERENT GROUP OF PEOPLE ... BUT THAT ITS MEMBERS ARE ALIVE TO THE NEEDS OF THE DAY AND THE TIMES IN WHICH WE LIVE ... AND ARE INTERESTED IN THE WELL BEING OF OUR TOWN AND OUR RESIDENTS.

4. **ON BEHALF OF OUR BOROUGH COUNCIL** I THANK YOU ALL WARMLY FOR THE WAY IN WHICH THIS TOAST HAS BEEN PROPOSED AND RECIEVED ... AND I WISH ALL THE MEMBERS OF THE CHAMBER OF TRADE AND COMMERCE EVERY SUCCESS AND PROSPERITY IN THE FUTURE ...

(d) Speech at election of new President of Literary and Scientific Society.

MADAM PRESIDENT, LADIES AND GENTLEMEN,

1. **FIRST OF ALL** ... LET ME CONGRATULATE YOU ... MADAM PRESIDENT ... ON THE DISTINCTION CONFERRED ON YOU TONIGHT BY THE MILNROW LITERARY AND SCIENTIFIC SOCIETY ... I KNOW IT IS AN HONOUR WHICH HAS BEEN WELL AND TRULY MERITED AND IS IN LINE WITH THE KENNEY FAMILY TRADITION ... FOR YOUR LATE HUSBAND JOHN ... AND YOUR SON ROGER WHO IS HERE TONIGHT ... HAVE BOTH HELD THIS HIGH OFFICE.

2. **IT IS VERY PLEASING TO ME** ... A FRIEND OF YOURS OF LONG STANDING ... TO SEE YOUR SERVICE TO THE SOCIETY ACKNOWLEDGED IN THIS WAY ... I HOPE YOU WILL BE BLESSED WITH GOOD HEALTH AND STAMINA TO ENABLE YOU TO CARRY OUT YOUR DUTIES AND THAT YOU WILL FIND YOUR PERIOD OF OFFICE AS PRESIDENT ... REWARDING AND ENJOYABLE.

3. **I KNOW FOR CERTAIN** THAT YOUR SOCIETY WILL HAVE CAUSE TO BE GRATEFUL TO YOU FOR YOUR GOODWILL AND DIGNIFIED LEADERSHIP.

4. **I MUST SAY** HOW PRIVILEGED I FEEL AT BEING INVITED TO BE PRESENT ON SUCH AN IMPORTANT OCCASION ... I'M ALSO NOT A LITTLE SURPRISED TO FIND MYSELF ADDRESSING SUCH AN AUGUST BODY OF PEOPLE.

5.   **I WAS BORN AND BROUGHT UP** IN THIS AREA AND IN FACT LIVED HERE ... APART FROM A PERIOD DURING THE WAR YEARS ... UNTIL 1950. MY FAMILY HAVE REMAINED IN AND AROUND THE AREA SO I HAVE BEEN A REGULAR VISITOR AND HAVE FREQUENTLY HEARD OF AND READ ABOUT YOUR LEARNED SOCIETY WHICH HAS BEEN ACTIVE FOR FIFTY EIGHT YEARS NOW.

6.   **DURING THAT PERIOD OF TIME** ... THE HEY-DAY OF THE CINEMA HAS BEEN AND GONE ... YET YOUR SOCIETY HAS SURVIVED ... AND DURING THAT TIME WE HAVE SEEN THAT MIXED BLESSING—THE BOX—INVADE ALL OUR HOMES AND CONFINE AUDIENCES TO THEIR ARMCHAIR EVENING AFTER EVENING WATCHING GOOD ... BAD ... AND INDIFFERENT TELEVISION PROGRAMMES ... AND YET YOUR SOCIETY HAS CONTINUED TO FLOURISH ... AND THANK GOODNESS YOUR SOCIETY AND SIMILAR GROUPS HAVE STAYED ALIVE ... THE COMMUNITY OWES YOU A DEBT OF GRATITUDE FOR THE STIMULATION YOU HAVE PROVIDED AND CONTINUE TO PROVIDE ... YOU ARE THE PERFECT ANTIDOTE TO SOAP OPERA AND CANNED RUBBISH ...

7.   **AS WE MOVE ON** INTO THE NEW WORLD OF HIGH TECHNOLOGY AND MICROCHIPS WITH ROBOTS DOING JOBS PREVIOUSLY DONE BY MEN AND WOMEN ... GROUPS SUCH AS YOURS WILL SURELY COME TO THE FOREFRONT TO PROVIDE THE MENTAL STIMULUS PEOPLE WILL NEED ... BECAUSE I DO NOT BELIEVE THESE LARGE NEW

161

LEISURE CENTRES WHICH ARE MUSHROOMING ALL OVER THE COUNTRY AT VAST EXPENSE FROM OUR TAXES AND RATES ... ARE GOING TO SOLVE ALL THE PROBLEMS OF THE INCREASED LEISURE TIME WHICH IS GOING TO BE AVAILABLE TO THE WORKING POPULATION OR TO THE UNEMPLOYED ... I BELIEVE THAT MORE AND MORE PEOPLE WILL TURN TO YOUR TYPE OF ORGANISATION TO SEEK TO WIDEN THEIR HORIZONS AND GAIN MENTAL DEVELOPMENT ... AND I KNOW THEY WILL NOT BE DISAPPOINTED.

8. **MADAM PRESIDENT, LADIES AND GENTLEMEN** . . .. I HAVE GREAT PLEASURE IN WISHING YOUR SOCIETY MANY MORE SUCCESSFUL YEARS ... AND THANK YOU ALL FOR YOUR WELCOME TO ME TONIGHT ...

(e) Speech at opening of Christmas Fair.

MR. SCOTT, LADIES AND GENTLEMEN, BOYS AND GIRLS.

1. **I WAS VERY PLEASED** WHEN I RECEIVED MR. SCOTT'S LETTER INVITING ME TO OPEN YOUR CHRISTMAS FAIR AND I AM DELIGHTED TO BE WITH YOU AND TO SEE SO MANY PEOPLE PRESENT ... SOME OF YOU FRIENDS FROM THE DAYS WHEN I SHARED WORSHIP AND FELLOWSHIP HERE ... SOME NOT SO FAMILIAR.

2. **I MUST COMPLIMENT** YOU ON THIS FINE NEW HALL ... WHICH I AM SEEING FOR THE FIRST TIME AND WHICH IS A FAR CRY FROM THE OLD HOLMES STREET PREMISES.

3. **ALTHOUGH IT IS MORE** THAN THIRTY YEARS SINCE I MOVED AWAY FROM THIS AREA ... I ALWAYS THINK OF MYSELF AS BELONGING TO ST. GEORGE'S AND I HAVE RETAINED MY INTEREST IN ALL YOUR ACTIVITIES ... NOT ONLY BECAUSE I STILL TAKE YOUR MAGAZINE ... BUT NOW THROUGH MY TWO GREAT NIECES ALISON AND CLAIRE WHO ARE MEMBERS OF YOUR GUIDES ... AND HERE TODAY ON THE GUIDE STALL.

4. **I KNOW SOMETHING** OF THE HARD WORK WHICH HAS GONE INTO MAKING THESE STALLS SO ATTRACTIVE AND WELL STOCKED AND I HOPE YOU ALL FIND LOTS OF THINGS TO BUY FOR CHRISTMAS PRESENTS SO THAT AT THE END OF THE AFTERNOON YOU WILL HAVE RAISED A GOODLY SUM TOWARDS YOUR DIOCESAN QUOTA . . .

5. **WITHOUT DETAINING** YOU ANY LONGER ... I HAVE PLEASURE IN DECLARING ST. GEORGE'S CHRISTMAS FAIR OPEN AND WISH ALL CONNECTED WITH IT EVERY POSSIBLE SUCCESS.

Aide-memoire for the above speech

1. PLEASURE BEING INVITED.
2. NEW HALL.
3. CONNECTION WITH ST. GEORGE'S.
4. CONGRATULATIONS HARD WORK.
5. SUCCESS TO FAIR, etc.

Appendix B

LETTERS AFTER NAMES

A.A.A.I.	Associate of the Institute of Administrative Accountants
A.A.C.P.	Associate of the Association of Computer Professionals.
A.A.D.C.	Air Aide-de-Camp.
A.A.I.A.	Associate of the Association of International Accountants.
A.A.M.S.	Associate Member of the Association of Medical Secretaries, Practice Administrators and Receptionists.
A.B.	Able Seaman
A.B.S.C.	Associate of the British Society of Commerce.
A.C.A.	Associate of the Institute of Chartered Accountants.
A.Cert.C.M.	The Archbishop of Canterbury's Certificate in Church Music.
A.C.G.I.	Associate of the City and Guilds of London Institute.
A.C.I.S.	Associate of the Chartered Institute of Secretaries and Administrators.
A.C.M.A.	Associate of the Institute of Cost and Management Accountants.
A.D.C.	Aide-de-Camp.
A.D.C.M.	The Archbishop of Canterbury's Diploma in Church Music.
A.D.I.	Approved Driving Instructor.
A.F.A.S.	Associate of the Faculty of Architects and Surveyors.
A.F.C.	Air Force Cross
A.F.C.S.	Associate of the Faculty of Secretaries.
A.F.M.	Air Force Medal.

A.F.T.Com.	Associate of the Faculty of Teachers in Commerce.
A.G.S.M.	Associate of the Guildhall School of Music and Drama.
A.H.A.	Associate of the Institute of Health Service Administrators.
A.H.C.I.M.A.	Associate of the Hotel, Catering and Institutional Management Association.
A.I.A.	Associate of the Institute of Actuaries.
A.I.B.	Associate of the Institute of Bankers.
A.I.L.	Associate of the Institute of Linguists.
A.I.M.	Associate of the Institute of Marketing.
A.Inst.T.A.	Associate of the Institute of Transport Administration.
A.I.P.	Associate of the Institute of Plumbing.
A.I.P.M.	Associate of the Institute of Personnel Management.
A.I.R.T.E.	Associate of the Institute of Road Transport Engineers.
A.I.S.T.D.	Associate of the Imperial Society of Teachers of Dancing.
A.I.T.S.A.	Associate of the Institute of Trading Standards Administration.
A.K.C.	Associateship of King's College, University of London.
A.L.A.	Associate of the Library Association.
A.L.C.M.	Associate of the London College of Music.
A.M.B.C.S.	Associate Member of the British Computer Society.
A.M.I.C.E.	Associate Member of the Institution of Civil Engineers.
A.M.I.E.E.	Associate Member of the Institution of Electrical Engineers.
A.M.I.M.I.	Associate Member of the Institute of the Motor Industry.
A.M.I.Struct.E.	Associate Member of the Institution of Structural Engineers.

A.M.I.T.D.	Associate Member of the Institute of Training and Development.
A.M.I.W.P.C.	Associate Member of the Institute of Water Pollution Control.
A.M.N.I.	Associate Member of the Nautical Institute.
A.M.R.S.H.	Associate Member of the Royal Society of Health.
A.Mus.L.C.M.	Associate in Music of the London College of Music.
A.Mus.T.C.L.	Associate in Music of Trinity College of Music, London.
A.M.W.E.S.	Associate Member of the Women's Engineering Society.
A.N.A.E.A.	Associate Member of the National Association of Estate Agents.
A.R.A.	Associate of the Royal Academy of Arts.
A.R.A.D.	Associate of the Royal Academy of Dancing.
A.R.A.M.	Associate of the Royal Academy of Music.
A.R.C.M.	Associate of the Royal College of Music.
A.R.C.O.	Associate of the Royal College of Organists.
A.R.I.B.A.	Associate of the Royal Institute of British Architects.
A.R.I.C.	Associateship of the Royal Institute of Chemistry.
A.R.I.C.S.	Associate of the Royal Institution of Chartered Surveyors.
A.R.I.P.H.H.	Associate of the Royal Institute of Public Health and Hygiene.
A.R.P.S.	Associate of the Royal Photographic Society.
A.R.R.C.	Associate of the Royal Red Cross.
A.R.S.C.M.	Associate Member of the Royal School of Church Music.
A.R.V.A.	Associate of the Rating and Valuation Association.

A.S.B.Th.	Associate of the Society of Health and Beauty Therapists.
A.S.C.A.	Associate of the Society of Company and Commercial Accountants.
A.S.C.T.	Associate Member of the Society of Commercial Teachers.
A.S.E.	Associate of the Society of Engineering.
A.S.I.A.	Associate of the Society of Investment Analysts.
A.S.L.C.	Advanced Secretarial Language Certificate.
Ass.I.P.H.E.	Associate of the Institution of Public Health Engineers.
A.S.T.A.	Associate of the Swimming Teachers Association.
A.S.V.A.	Associate of the Incorporated Society of Valuers and Auctioneers.
A.T.C.	Art Teachers Certificate.
A.T.D.	Art Teachers Diploma.
A.T.I.	Associate of the Textile Institute.
A.T.P.L.	Airline Transport Pilot's Licence.
B.A.	Bachelor of Arts.
B.Ac.	Bachelor of Acupuncture.
B.A.(Econ)	Bachelor of Arts in Economics and Social Studies.
B.A.(Ed).	Bachelor of Arts (Education).
B.Agr.	Bachelor of Agriculture.
B.A.(Lan).	Bachelor of Languages.
B.A.(Law)	Bachelor of Arts in Law.
B.A.O.	Bachelor of Obstetrics.
B.Arch.	Bachelor of Architecture.
B.Ch.D.	Bachelor of Dental Surgery.
B.Chir.	Bachelor of Surgery.
B.C.L.	Bachelor of Civil Law.

B.Com.	Bachelor of Commerce.
B.D.	Bachelor of Divinity.
B.D.S.	Bachelor of Dental Surgery.
B.Ed.	Bachelor of Education.
B.E.M.	British Empire Medal.
B.Eng.	Bachelor of Engineering.
B.Eng.(Tech.)	Bachelor of Engineering (Technology).
B.F.A.	Bachelor of Fine Arts.
B.H.S.I.	British Horse Society's Instructor's Certificate.
B.L.D.	Bachelor of Landscape Design.
B.L.E.	Bachelor of Land Economy.
B.Lib.	Bachelor of Librarianship.
B.Ling.	Bachelor of Linguistics.
B.Litt.	Bachelor of Letters.
B.L.S.	Bachelor of Library Studies.
B.M.	Bachelor of Medicine.
B.M.,B.Ch.	Conjoint degree of Bachelor of Medicine, Bachelor of Surgery. Oxford University.
B.M.,B.S.	Conjoint degree of Bachelor of Medicine, Bachelor of Surgery. Nottingham University.
B.Med.Biol.	Bachelor of Medical Biology.
B.Med.Sci.	Bachelor of Medical Science.
B.Med.Sci.(Speech)	Bachelor of Medical Science (Speech).
B.Met.	Bachelor of Metallurgy.
B.M.Sc.	Bachelor of Medical Science.
B.Mus.	Bachelor of Music.
B.N.	Bachelor of Nursing.
B.N.Nursing Studies	Bachelor of Nursing, Nursing Studies.
B.Pharm.	Bachelor of Pharmacy.
B.Phil.	Bachelor of Philosophy.
B.Phil.(Ed.)	Bachelor of Philosophy (Education).
B.P.L.	Bachelor of Planning.

169

B.Sc.	Bachelor of Science.
B.Sc.Agr.	Bachelor of Science in Agriculture.
B.Sc.(Architecture)	Bachelor of Science (Architecture)
B.Sc.(Dent.Sci.)	Bachelor of Science in Dental Science.
B.Sc.Econ.	Bachelor of the Faculty of Economic and Social Studies.
B.Sc.(Econ.)	Bachelor of Science in Economics.
B.Sc.Eng.	Bachelor of Science in Engineering.
B.Sc.For.	Bachelor of Science in Forestry.
B.Sc.(Med.Sc.)	Bachelor of Science (Medical Sciences).
B.Sc.(Social Sc.)	Bachelor of Science (Social Sciences).
B.Sc.Tech.	Bachelor of Technical Science.
B.Sc.(Town and Regional Planning)	Bachelor of Science (Town and Regional Planning).
B.Soc.Sci.	Bachelor of Social Science.
B.S.S.G.	Member of the British Society of Scientific Glassblowers.
B.Tech.	Bachelor of Technology.
B.T.E.C.H.C.	Business and Technician Education Council Higher Certificate.
B.T.E.C.H.D.	Business and Technician Education Council Higher Diploma.
B.T.E.C.H.N.C.	Business and Technician Education Council Higher National Certificate.
B.T.E.C.H.N.D.	Business and Techician Education Council Higher National Diploma.
B.T.E.C.N.C.	Business and Technician Education Council National Certificate.
B.T.E.C.N.D.	Business and Technician Education Council National Diploma.
B.Th.	Bachelor of Theology.
B.T.P.	Bachelor of Town and Country Planning.
B.Vet.Med.	Bachelor of Veterinary Medicine.
B.V.M.& S.	Bachelor of Veterinary Medicine and Surgery. (Univ. of Edinburgh).

170

B.V.M.S.	Bachelor of Veterinary Medicine and Surgery. (Univ. of Glasgow).
B.V.Sc.	Bachelor of Veterinary Science.
Bt. or Bart.	Baronet.
C.A.	Member of the Institute of Chartered Accountants of Scotland.
C.A.S.	Certification of Accountancy Studies.
C.A.S.S.	Certificate of Applied Social Studies.
C.A.T.	Certificate for Accounting Technicians.
C.B.	Companion of the Order of the Bath.
C.B.E.	Commander of the Order of the British Empire.
C.B.I.M.	Companion of the British Institute of Management.
C.Biol.	Chartered Biologist.
C.C.	Common Councillor, i.e. Member of the Court of the Common Council of the Corporation of London.
C.Chem.	Chartered Chemist.
C.Col.	Chartered Colourist.
C.Dip.A.F.	Certified Diploma in Accounting and Finance.
C.Eng.	Chartered Engineer.
C.Eng.F.I.Mech.E.	Fellow of the Institution of Mechanical Engineers.
C.Eng.F.I.Prod.E.	Fellow of the Institution of Production Engineers.
C.Eng.M.I.Mech.E.	Member of the Institution of Mechanical Engineers.
C.Eng.M.I.Prod.E.	Member of the Institution of Production Engineers.
Cert.B.D.S.	Special Category Membership of the British Display Society.
Cert.Bib.Know.	Certificate of Bible Knowledge.

171

APPENDIX B

Cert.Ds.R.C.A.	Certificate in Design, Royal College of Art.
Cert.H.S.A.P.	Certificate in Health Service Administration Practice.
Cert.H.S.M.	Certificate in Health Service Management.
Cert.Occ.Hyg.	Certificate of Operational Competence in Comprehensive Occupational Hygiene.
C.E.T.H.V.	Certificate of Education in Training as Health Visitor.
C.F.	Chaplain to the Forces.
C.G.M.	Conspicuous Gallantry Medal.
C.H.	Companion of Honour.
Ch.B.	Bachelor of Surgery.
C.H.M.	Choir-Training Diploma of the Royal College of Organists.
Ch.M.	Master of Surgery.
C.H.P.	Certificate in Hypnosis and Psychology.
C.I.Agr.E.	Companion of the Institution of Agricultural Engineers.
C.I.E.	Companion of the Order of the Indian Empire.
C.I.M.G.Tech.E.	Companion of the Institution of Mechanical and General Technician Engineers.
C.I.O.C.	Craftsman of the Institute of Carpenters.
C.L.(A.D.O.)	Diploma in Contact Lens Fitting of the Assocation of Dispensing Opticians.
C.M.A.	Certificate in Management Accountancy.
C.M.B.H.I.	Craft Member of the British Horological Institute.
C.M.G.	Companion of the Order of St. Michael and St. George.
C.M.I.W.H.T.E.	Companion Member of the Institution of Works and Highways Technician Engineers.
C.M.I.W.Sc.	Certified Member of the Institute of Wood Science.

C.M.S.	Certificate in Management Studies.
Comp.I.A.P.	Companion of the Institution of Analysts and Programmers.
Comp.I.E.E.	Companion of the Institution of Electrical Engineers.
Comp.I.Gas E.	Companion of Institution of Gas Engineers.
Comp.I.P.	Companion of the Institute of Plumbing.
Comp.S.L.E.A.T.	Companion of the Society of Licensed Aircraft Engineers and Technologists.
C.P.A.	Chartered Patent Agent.
C.P.C.	Certificate of Professional Competence, Institute of Transport Administration.
C.Phys.	Chartered Physicist of the Institute of Physics.
C.P.L.	Commercial Pilot's Licence.
C.P.S.	Certificate in Pastoral Studies and Applied Theology.
C.P.V.E.	Certificate of Pre-Vocational Education.
C.Q.S.W.	Certificate of Qualification in Social Work.
C.R.N.C.M.	Companion of the Royal Northern College of Music.
C.S.I.	Companion of the Order of the Star of India.
C.S.S.	Certificate in Social Service.
C.V.O.	Commander of the Royal Victorian Order.
D.A.	Diploma in Anaesthetics.
D.A.E.S.	Diploma in Advanced Educational Studies.
D.Arch.	Diploma in Architecture.
D.Av.Med.	Diploma in Aviation Medicine.
D.B.E.	Dame Commander of the Order of the British Empire.
D.B.O.	Diploma of the British Orthoptic Society.
D.C.B.	Dame Commander of the Bath.
D.C.C.	Diploma of Chelsea College.

173

D.C.D.H.	Diploma in Child Dental Health.
D.C.G.	Diploma in Careers Guidance.
D.C.H.	Diploma in Child Health.
D.Ch.D.	Doctor of Dental Surgery.
D.C.H.T.	Diploma in Community Health in Tropical Countries.
D.C.L.	Doctor of Civil Laws.
D.C.L.F.	Diploma in Contact Lens Fitting.
D.C.L.P.	Diploma in Contact Lens Practice.
D.C.M.	Distinguished Conduct Medal.
D.C.M.G.	Dame Commander of St. Michael and St. George.
D.C.R.M.U.	Diploma of the College of Radiographers in Medical Ultra Sound.
D.C.R.	Diploma of the College of Radiographers.
D.C.R.R.N.I.	Diploma of the College of Radiographers in Radionuclide Imaging.
D.C.V.O.	Dame Commander of the Royal Victorian Order.
D.D.	Doctor of Divinity.
D.D.H.(Birm.)	Diploma in Dental Health, University of Birmingham.
D.D.Orth.R.C.P.S. Glas.	Diploma in Dental Orthopaedics of the Royal College of Physicians and Surgeons of Glasgow.
D.D.P.H.	Diploma in Dental Public Health.
D.D.S.	Doctor of Dental Surgery.
D.D.Sc.	Doctor of Dental Science.
D.Eng.	Doctor of Engineering.
D.F.C.	Distinguished Flying Cross.
D.F.M.	Distinguished Flying Medal.
D.H.E.	Diploma in Horticulture, Royal Botanic Gardens, Edinburgh.
D.H.M.S.A.	Diploma in History of Medicine, Society of Apothecaries.

D.H.P.	Diploma in Hypnosis and Psychotherapy.
D.I.A.	Diploma in Industrial Administration.
D.I.H.	Diploma in Industrial Health.
D.L.	Deputy Lieutenant.
Dip.A.D.	Diploma in Art and Design.
Dip.A.E.	Diploma in Adult Education.
D.Agr.Comm.	Diploma in Agricultural Communication.
Dip.Arch.	Diploma in Architecture.
Dip.B.A.	Diploma in Business Adminstration.
Dip.C.A.M.	Diploma of the Communication Advertising and Marketing Education Foundation.
Dip.C.D.	Diploma in Community Development.
Dip.Clin.Path.	Diploma in Clinical Pathology.
Dip.C.O.T.	Diploma of the College of Occupational Therapists.
Dip.C.T.	Diploma of Corporate Treasury Management.
Dip.Ed.	Diploma in Education.
Dip.E.F.	Diploma in Executive Finance.
Dip.E.H.	Diploma in Environmental Health.
Dip.E.M.A.	Diploma in Executive Finance for non-Accountants.
Dip.Eng.Lit.	Diploma in English Literature.
Dip.F.D.	Diploma in Funeral Directing.
Dip.F.S.	Financial Studies Diploma
Dip.G.A.I.	Diploma of the Guild of Architectual Ironmongers.
Dip.G.S.M.	Diploma of the Guildhall School of Music and Drama.
Dip.I.B.(Scot.)	Diplomate of the Institute of Bankers in Scotland.
Dip.L.E.	Diploma in Land Economy.
Dip.M.	Diploma in Marketing, Institute of Marketing.

Dip.Occ.Hyg.	Diploma of Professional Competence in Comphrehensive Occupational Hygiene.
Dip.Pharm.Med.	Diploma in Pharmaceutical Medicine.
Dip.Phil.	Diploma in Philosophy.
Dip.R.A.M.	Diploma of the Royal Academy of Music.
Dip.R.C.M.	Diploma of the Royal College of Music.
Dip.R.G.R.	Diploma of the Society of Remedial Gymnastics and Recreational Therapy.
Dip.R.M.S.	Diploma of the Royal Microscopical Society.
Dip.Sc.	Diploma in Science.
Dip.T.E.	Diploma in Transportation Engineering.
Dip.T.E.S.O.L.	Diploma in Teaching English to Speakers of Other Languages.
Dip.T.M.	Diploma in Training Management.
Dip.Ven.	Diploma in Venereology.
Dip.W.C.F.	Diploma of the Worshipful Company of Farriers.
Dip.Y.D.	Diploma of Youth Development.
D.I.S.	Diploma in Industrial Studies.
D.Lit.	Doctor of Letters or Literature.
D.L.O.	Diploma of Laryngology and Otology.
D.L.P.	Diploma in Legal Practice.
D.M.	Doctor of Medicine.
D.Med.Rehab.	Diploma in Medical Rehabilitation.
D.Met.	Doctor of Metallurgy.
D.M.J.(Clin.)	Diploma in Medical Jurisprudence (Clinical)
D.M.J.(Path.)	Diploma in Medical Jurisprudence (Pathological)
D.M.R.D.	Diploma in Medical Radio Diagnosis.
D.M.R.T.	Diploma in Radiotherapy.
D.M.S.	Diploma in Management Studies.
D.Mus.	Doctor of Music.

D.Mus.Cantuar.	The Archbishop of Canterbury's Doctorate in Music.
D.O.	Diploma in Ophthalmology.
D.O.	Diploma in Osteopathy.
D.Opt.	Diploma in Ophthalmic Optics.
D.Orth.	Diploma in Orthoptics.
D.Orth.R.C.S.Eng.	Diplomate in Orthodontics, Royal College of Surgeons of England.
D.P.A.	Diploma in Public Administration.
Dp.Bact.	Diploma in Bacteriology.
D.P.D.	Diploma in Public Dentistry.
D.P.H.	Diploma in Public Health.
D.Phil.	Doctor of Philosophy.
D.P.H.R.C.S.Eng.	Diploma in Dental Public Health, Royal College of Surgeons of England.
D.P.M.	Diploma in Psychological Medicine.
D.P.S.	Diploma in Pastoral Studies and Applied Theology. Aberbeen University.
D.P.S.	Diploma in Professional Studies, Loughborough University of Technology.
D.P.S.E.	Diploma in Professional Studies in Education.
Dr.Ac.	Doctor of Acupuncture.
D.R.C.O.G.	Diploma of the Royal College of Obstetricians and Gynaecologists.
D.R.D.R.C.S.Ed.	Diploma in Restorative Dentistry, Royal College of Surgeons of Edinburgh.
D.R.E.	Diploma in Remedial Electrolysis, Institute of Electrolysis.
Dr.(R.C.A.)	Doctor of the Royal College of Art.
D.R.S.A.M.	Diploma of the Royal Scottish Academy of Music and Drama.
D.Sc.	Doctor of Science.
D.S.C.	Distinguished Service Cross.

177

D.S.Econ.	Doctor in the Faculty of Economics and Social Studies.
D.Sc.(Econ.)	Doctor of Science (Economics).
D.Sc.(Eng.)	Doctor of Science (Engineering).
D.Sc.(Soc.Scs.)	Doctor of Science in the Social Sciences.
D.Sc.Tech.	Doctor of Technical Science.
D.Sc.Sc.	Doctor of Social Science.
D.S.M.	Distinguished Service Medal.
D.S.O.	Distinguished Service Order.
D.S.T.A.	Diploma Member of the Swimming Teachers' Association.
D.T.C.D.	Diploma in Tuberculosis and Chest Diseases.
D.T.C.H.	Diploma in Tropical Child Health.
D.Tech.	Doctor of Technology.
D.T.M.&H.	Diploma in Tropical Medicine and Hygiene.
D.Vet.Med.	Doctor of Veterinary Medicine, University of London.
D.V.M.	Doctor of Veterinary Medicine, University of Glasgow.
D.V.M.&S.	Doctor of Veterinary Medicine and Surgery, University of Edinburgh.
D.V.S.	Doctor of Veterinary Surgery.
D.V.Sc.	Doctor of Veterinary Science.
E.N.	Enrolled Nurse.
E.N.(G).	Enrolled Nurse (General)
Eng.Tech.	Engineering Technician.
E.N.(M.)	Enrolled Nurse (Mental).
E.N.(M.H.)	Enrolled Nurse (Mental Handicap).
E.R.D.	Army Emergency Reserve Decoration.
F.A.A.I.	Fellow of the Institute of Administrative Accountants.

F.A.B.A.C.	Fellow of the Association of Business and Administrative Computing.
F.A.B.E.	Fellow of the Association of Business Executives.
F.Ac.A.	Fellow of the Acupuncture Association.
F.A.C.P.	Fellow of the Association of Computer Professionals.
F.A.D.O.	Fellow of the Association of Dispensing Opticians.
F.A.D.O.(Hons.)	Fellow of the Association of Dispensing Opticians with Honours Diploma.
F.A.D.O.(Hons.)C.L.	Fellow of the Association of Dispensing Opticians with Honours Diploma in Contact Lens Fitting.
F.A.I.A.	Fellow of the Association of International Accountants.
F.A.I.E.	Fellow of the British Association of Industrial Editors.
F.A.M.S.	Fellow of the Association of Medical Secretaries, Practice Administrators and Receptionists.
F.A.N.Y.	First Aid Nursing Yeomanry.
F.A.S.I.	Fellow of the Ambulance Service Institute.
F.B.A.	Fellow of the British Academy.
F.B.A.	Fellow of the British Arts Association.
F.B.B.O.	Fellow of the British Ballet Organisation.
F.B.C.O.	Fellow of the British College of Ophthalmic Opticians.
F.B.C.S.	Fellow of the British Computer Society.
F.B.E.I.	Fellow of the Institution of Body Engineers.
F.B.H.A.	Fellow of the British Hypnotherapy Association.
F.B.H.I.	Fellow of the British Horological Institute.
F.B.H.S.	Fellow of the British Horse Society.
F.B.I.D.	Fellow of the British Institute of Interior Design.

179

F.B.I.E.	Fellow of the British Institute of Embalmers.
F.B.I.M.	Fellow of the British Institute of Management.
F.B.I.P.F.	Fellow of the British Institute of Professional Photography.
F.B.I.S.	Fellow of the British Interplanetary Society.
F.B.I.S.T.	Fellow of the British Institute of Surgical Technologists.
F.B.O.A.	Fellow of the British Optical Association.
F.B.Ps.S.	Fellow of the British Psychological Society.
F.B.S.C.	Fellow of the British Society of Commerce.
F.B.T.	Fellow of the Association of Beauty Teachers.
F.C.A.	Fellow of the Institute of Chartered Accountants in England and Wales.
F.C.A.A.	Fellow of the Faculty of Community Accountancy and Administration.
F.C.A.M.	Fellow of the Communication Advertising and Marketing Education Foundation.
F.C.B.S.I.	Fellow of the Chartered Building Societies Institute.
F.C.C.A.	Fellow of the Chartered Association of Certified Accountants.
F.C.E.A.	Fellow of the Association of Cost and Executive Accountants.
F.C.F.I.	Fellow of the Clothing and Footwear Institute.
F.Ch.S.	Fellow of the Society of Chiropodists.
F.C.I.	Fellow of the Institute of Commerce.
F.C.I.Arb.	Fellow of the Chartered Institute of Arbitrators.
F.C.I.B.S.	Fellow of the Chartered Institution of Building Services.
F.C.I.I.	Fellow of the Chartered Insurance Institute.
F.C.I.L.A.	Fellow of the Chartered Institute of Loss Adjusters.

F.C.I.O.B.	Fellow of the Chartered Institute of Building.
F.C.I.S.	Fellow of the Institute of Chartered Secretaries and Administrators.
F.C.I.T.	Fellow of the Chartered Institute of Transport.
F.C.M.A.	Fellow of the Institute of Cost and Management Accountants.
F.Coll.P.	Ordinary Fellow of the College of Preceptors.
F.C.P.	Fellow of the College of Preceptors.
F.C.P.M.	Fellow of the Confederation of Professional Management.
F.C.S.I.	Fellow of the Construction Surveyors' Institute.
F.C.S.P.	Fellow of the Chartered Society of Physiotherapy.
F.C.T.	Fellow of the Association of Corporate Treasurers.
F.D.S.R.C.P.S.Glas.	Fellow in Dental Surgery of the Royal College of Physicians and Surgeons of Glasgow.
F.D.S.R.C.S.Ed..	Fellow in Dental Surgery of the Royal College of Surgeons of Edinburgh.
F.D.S.R.C.S.Eng.	Fellow in Dental Surgery of the Royal College of Surgeons in England.
F.E.C.I.	Fellow of the Institute of Employment Consultants.
F.E.I.S.	Fellow of the Educational Institute of Scotland.
F.F.A.	Fellow of the Faculty of Actuaries.
F.F.A.R.C.S.Eng.	Fellow of the Faculty of Anaesthetists of the Royal College of Surgeons of England.
F.F.A.R.C.S.Ire.	Fellow of the Faculty of Anaesthetists, Royal College of Surgeons in Ireland.
F.F.A.S.	Fellow of the Faculty of Architects and Surveyors.

APPENDIX B

F.F.B.	Fellow of the Faculty of Building.
F.F.C.I.	Fellow of the Faculty of Commerce and Industry.
F.F.C.S.	Fellow of the Faculty of Secretaries.
F.F.D.O.	Fellow of the Faculty of Dispensing Opticians.
F.F.R.R.C.S.Irel.	Fellow of the Faculty of Radiologists, Royal College of Surgeons in Ireland.
F.F.S.	Fellow of the Faculty of Architects and Surveyors (Surveyors).
F.F.T.Com.	Fellow of the Faculty of Teachers in Commerce.
F.G.A.	Fellow of the Gemmological Association.
F.G.C.L.	Fellow of the Guild of Cleaners and Launderers.
F.G.I.	Fellow of the Greek Institute.
F.G.S.	Fellow of the Geological Society of London.
F.G.S.M.	Fellow of the Guildhall School of Music and Drama.
F.H.A.	Fellow of the Institute of Health Service Administrators.
F.H.C.I.M.A.	Fellow of the Hotel, Catering and Institutional Management Association.
F.H.G.	Fellow of the Institute of Heraldic and Genealogical Studies.
F.H.T.T.A.	Fellow of the Highway and Traffic Technicians Association.
F.I.A.	Fellow of the Institute of Actuaries.
F.I.A.A.	Fellow of the Incorporated Assocation of Architects and Surveyors (Architect).
F.I.A.E.A.	Fellow of the Institute of Automotive Engineer Assessors.
F.I.Agr.E.	Fellow of the Institution of Agricultural Engineers.
F.I.A.P.	Fellow of the Institution of Analysts and Programmers.

F.I.A.S.	Fellow of the Incorporated Assocation of Architects and Surveyors (Surveyor).
F.I.A.T.	Fellow of the Institute of Animal Technicians.
F.I.A.T.	Fellow of the Institute of Asphalt Technology.
F.I.B.	Fellow of the Institute of Bankers.
F.I.B.A.	Fellow of the Institution of Business Agents.
F.I.B.C.O.	Fellow of the Institution of Building Control Officers.
F.I.B.F.	Fellow of the Institute of British Foundrymen.
F.I.Biol.	Fellow of the Institute of Biology.
F.I.B.(Scot.)	Fellow of the Institute of Bankers in Scotland.
F.I.C.D.	Fellow of the Institute of Creative Design.
F.I.C.E.	Fellow of the Institution of Civil Engineers.
F.I.Chem.E.	Fellow of the Institution of Chemical Engineers.
F.I.C.M.	Fellow of the Institute of Credit Management.
F.I.C.O.	Fellow of the Institute of Careers Officers.
F.I.Corr.S.T.	Fellow of the Institution of Corrosion Science and Technology.
F.I.C.S.	Fellow of the Institute of Chartered Shipbrokers.
F.I.C.W.	Fellow of the Institute of Clerks of Works.
F.I.D.T.A.	Fellow of the International Dance Teachers' Assocation.
F.I.E.D.	Fellow of the Institution of Engineering Designers.
F.I.E.E.	Fellow of the Institution of Electrical Engineers.
F.I.Elec.I.E.	Fellow of the Institution of Electrical and Electronics Incorporated Engineers.
F.I.E.M.	Fellow of the Institute of Executives and Managers.

183

F.I.E.R.E.	Fellow of the Institution of Electronic and Radio Engineers.
F.I.Ex.	Fellow of the Institute of Export.
F.I.Ex.E.	Fellow of the Institute of Executive Engineers and Officers.
F.I.Exp.E.	Fellow of the Institute of Explosives Engineers.
F.I.Fire E.	Fellow of the Institution of Fire Engineers.
F.I.F.S.T.	Fellow of the Institute of Food Science and Technology.
F.I.GasE.	Fellow of the Institution of Gas Engineers.
F.I.G.D.	Fellow of the Institute of Grocery Distribution.
F.I.Geol.	Fellow of the Institution of Geologists.
F.I.H.	Fellow of the Institute of Housing.
F.I.H.Ec.	Fellow of the Institute of Home Economics.
F.I.H.E.	Fellow of the Institution of Highway Engineers.
F.I.H.T.C.M.	Fellow of the Institute of Hotel, Tourism and Catering Management.
F.I.I.M.	Fellow of the Institution of Industrial Managers.
F.I.Inst.Sc.	Fellow of the Institute of Information Scientists.
F.I.I.R.S.M.	Fellow of the International Institute of Risk and Safety Management.
F.I.I.S.E.	Fellow of the International Institute of Social Economics.
F.I.I.Sec.	Fellow of the Institute of Industrial Security.
F.I.L.	Fellow of the Institute of Linguists.
F.I.L.A.M.	Fellow of the Institute of Leisure and Amenity Management.
F.I.M.	Fellow of the Institute of Metals.
F.I.M.A.	Fellow of the Institute of Mathematics and its Applications.
F.I.Manf.	Fellow of the Institute of Manufacturing.

F.I.Mar.E.	Fellow of the Institute of Marine Engineers.
F.I.M.B.I.	Fellow of the Institute of Medical and Biological Illustration.
F.I.M.B.M.	Fellow of the Institute of Municipal Building Management.
F.I.M.C.	Fellow of the Institute of Management Consultants.
F.I.Mech.E.	Fellow of the Institution of Mechanical Engineers.
F.I.M.F.	Fellow of the Institute of Metal Finishing.
F.I.M.G.Tech.E.	Fellow of the Institution of Mechanical and General Technician Engineers.
F.I.M.H.	Fellow of the Institute of Materials Handling.
F.I.M.I.	Fellow of the Institute of the Motor Industry.
F.I.Min.E.	Fellow of the Institution of Mining Engineers.
F.I.M.I.T.	Fellow of the Institute of Musical Instrument Technology.
F.I.M.L.S.	Fellow of the Institute of Medical Laboratory Sciences.
F.I.M.M.	Fellow of the Institute of Male Masseurs.
F.I.M.M.	Fellow of the Institution of Mining and Metallurgy.
F.I.M.S.	Fellow of the Institute of Management Specialists.
F.I.Mun.E.	Fellow of the Institution of Municipal Engineers.
F.Inst.A.E.A.	Fellow of the Institue of Automotive Engineer Assessors.
F.Inst.A.M.	Fellow of the Institute of Administrative Management.
F.Inst.B.B.	Fellow of the Institute of British Bakers.
F.Inst.B.C.A.	Fellow of the Institute of Burial and Cremation Administration.

F.Inst.B.R.M.	Fellow of the Institute of Baths and Recreation Management.
F.Inst.B.T.M.	Fellow of the Institute of Business and Technical Management.
F.Inst.Ch.	Fellow of the Institute of Chiropodists.
F.Inst.C.M.	Fellow of the Institute of Commercial Management.
F.Inst.E.	Fellow of the Institute of Energy.
F.Inst.F.F.	Fellow of the Institute of Freight Forwarders.
F.Inst.L.Ex.	Fellow of the Institute of Legal Executives.
F.Inst.M.	Fellow of the Institute of Marketing.
F.Inst.M.C.	Fellow of the Institute of Measurement and Control.
F.Inst.M.E.	Fellow Member of the International Institute of Management Executives.
F.Inst.N.D.T.	Fellow of the British Institute of Non-Destructive Testing.
F.Inst.P.	Fellow of the Institute of Physics.
F.Inst.Pet.	Fellow of the Institute of Petroleum.
F.Inst.Pkg.	Fellow of the Institute of Packaging.
F.Inst.P.M.	Fellow of the Institute of Professional Managers.
F.Inst.P.S.	Fellow of the Institute of Purchasing and Supply.
F.Inst.R.	Fellow of the Institute of Refrigeration.
F.Inst.S.M.M.	Fellow of the Institute of Sales and Marketing Management.
F.Inst.T.A.	Fellow of the Institute of Transport Administration.
F.Inst.W.M.	Fellow of the Institute of Wastes Management.
F.I.O.C.	Fellow of the Institute of Carpenters.
F.I.P.	Fellow of the Institute of Plumbing.
F.I.O.P.	Fellow of the Institute of Printing.
F.I.P.A.	Fellow of the Institute of Practitioners in Advertising.

F.I.P.C.	Fellow of the Institute of Production Control.
F.I.P.H.E.	Fellow of the Institution of Public Health Engineers.
F.I.P.I.	Fellow of the Institute of Professional Investigators.
F.I.P.M.	Fellow of the Institute of Personnel Management.
F.I.P.R.	Fellow of the Institute of Public Relations.
F.I.Q.A.	Fellow of the Institute of Quality Assurance.
F.I.R.	Fellow of the Institute of Population Registration.
F.I.R.S.E.	Fellow of the Institute of Railway Signal Engineers.
F.I.R.T.	Fellow of the Institute of Reprographic Technology.
F.I.S.	Fellow of the Institute of Statisticians.
F.I.S.M.	Fellow of the Institute of Supervisory Management.
F.I.S.O.B.	Fellow of the Incorporated Society of Organ Builders.
F.I.S.T.	Fellow of the Institute of Science and Technology.
F.I.S.T.C.	Fellow of the Institute of Scientific and Technical Communicators.
F.I.S.T.C.	Fellow of the International Sports Therapy Council.
F.I.S.T.D.	Fellow of the Imperial Society of Teachers of Dancing.
F.I.S.T.M.	Fellow of the Institute of Sales Technology and Management.
F.I.Struct.E.	Fellow of the Institution of Structural Engineers.
F.I.S.W.	Fellow of the Institute of Social Welfare.
F.I.T.D.	Fellow of the Institute of Training and Development.
F.I.T.S.A.	Fellow of the Institute of Trading Standards Administration.

F.I.W.H.T.E.	Fellow of the Institutuion of Works and Highways Technician Engineers.
F.L.A.	Fellow of the Library Association.
F.L.C.M.	Fellow of the London College of Music.
F.L.C.S.P.	Fellow of the London and Counties Society of Physiologists.
F.L.I.	Fellow of the Landscape Institute.
F.L.S.	Fellow of the Linnean Society.
F.L.S.P.T.	Fellow of the London School of Polymer Technology.
F.M.A.	Fellow of the Museums Association.
F.M.P.A.	Fellow of the Master Photographers Association.
F.M.R.	Fellow of the Association of Health Care Information and Medical Records Officers.
F.M.S.	Fellow of the Institute of Management Services.
F.N.A.E.A.	Fellow of the National Association of Estate Agents.
F.N.I.	Fellow of the Nautical Institute.
F.N.I.H.	Fellow of the National Institute of Hardware.
F.N.I.M.H.	Fellow of the National Institute of Medical Herbalists.
F.P.M.I.	Fellow of the Pensions Management Institute.
F.P.R.I.	Fellow of the Plastics and Rubber Institute.
F.P.S.	Fellow of the Pharmaceutical Society.
F.R.Ae.S.	Fellow of the Royal Aeronautical Society.
F.R.A.M.	Fellow of the Royal Academy of Music.
F.R.A.S.	Fellow of the Royal Astronomical Society.
F.R.C.G.P.	Fellow of the Royal College of General Practitioners.
F.R.C.M.	Fellow of the Royal College of Music.

F.R.C.O.	Fellow of the Royal College of Organists.
F.R.C.O.G.	Fellow of the Royal College of Obstetricians and Gynaecologists.
F.R.C.P.	Fellow of the Royal College of Physicians.
F.R.C.Path.	Fellow of the Royal College of Pathologists.
F.R.C.Psych.	Fellow of the Royal College of Psychiatrists.
F.R.C.R.	Fellow of the Royal College of Radiologists.
F.R.C.S.Ed.	Fellow of the Royal College of Surgeons of Edinburgh.
F.R.C.S.Eng.	Fellow of the Royal College of Surgeons of England.
F.R.C.S.Glas.	Fellow of the Royal College of Physicians and Surgeons of Glasgow.
F.R.C.S.(Ire.).	Fellow of the Royal College of Surgeons in Ireland.
F.R.C.V.S.	Fellow of the Royal College of Veterinary Surgeons.
F.R.H.S.	Fellow of the Royal Horticultural Society.
F.R.I.B.A.	Fellow of the Royal Institute of British Architects.
F.R.I.C.S.	Fellow of the Royal Institution of Chartered Surveyors.
F.R.I.N.	Fellow of the Royal Institution of Navigation.
F.R.I.N.A.	Fellow of the Royal Institution of Naval Architects.
F.R.I.P.H.H.	Fellow of the Royal Institute of Public Health and Hygiene.
F.R.N.C.M.	Fellow of the Royal Northern College of Music.
F.R.P.S.	Fellow of the Royal Photographic Society.
F.R.S.	Fellow of the Royal Society.
F.R.S.C.	Fellow of the Royal Society of Chemistry.
F.R.S.C.M.	Fellow of the Royal School of Church Music.
F.R.S.H.	Fellow of the Royal Society of Health.

APPENDIX B

F.R.T.P.I.	Fellow of the Royal Town Planning Institute.
F.R.V.A.	Fellow of the Rating and Valuation Association.
F.S.A.O.	Fellow of the Scottish Association of Opticians.
F.S.B.P.	Fellow of the Society of Business Practitioners.
F.S.B.Th.	Fellow of the Society of Health and Beauty Therapists.
F.S.C.A.	Fellow of the Society of Company and Commercial Accountants.
F.S.C.P.	Fellow of the Society of Certified Professionals.
F.S.C.T.	Fellow of the Society of Cardiological Technicians.
F.S.C.T.	Fellow of the Society of Commercial Teachers.
F.S.D.C.	Fellow of the Society of Dyers and Colourists.
F.S.E.	Fellow of the Society of Engineers.
F.S.E.R.T.	Fellow of the Society of Electronic and Radio Technicians.
F.S.G.T.	Fellow of the Society of Glass Technology.
F.S.H.A.A.	Fellow of the Society of Hearing Aid Audiologists.
F.S.I.A.	Fellow of the Society of Investment Analysts.
F.S.I.A.D.	Fellow of the Society of Industrial Artists and Designers.
F.S.L.A.E.T.	Fellow of the Society of Licensed Aircraft Engineers and Technologists.
F.S.M.C.	Fellow of the Worshipful Company of Spectacle Makers.
F.S.R.G.	Fellow of the Society of Remedial Gymnasts.
F.S.S.	Fellow of the Royal Statistical Society.

F.S.T.A.	Fellow of the Swimming Teachers' Association.
F.S.V.A.	Fellow of the Incorporated Society of Valuers and Auctioneers.
F.T.C.L.	Fellow of Trinity College of Music, London.
F.T.I.	Fellow of the Textile Institute.
F.W.C.F.	Fellow of the Worshipful Company of Farriers.
F.Weld.I.	Fellow of the Welding Institute.
F.Y.D.	Fellowship of the Youth Development Association.
G.B.E.	Knight (or Dame) Grand Cross of the British Empire.
G.B.S.M.	Graduate of Birmingham School of Music.
G.C.	George Cross.
G.C.B.	Knight (or Dame) Grand Cross of the Bath.
G.C.M.G.	Knight (or Dame) Grand Cross of St. Michael and St. George.
G.C.V.O.	Knight (or Dame) Grand Cross of the Royal Victorian Order.
G.G.S.M.	Graduate Diploma of the Guildhall School of Music and Drama.
G.I.M.I.	Graduate of the Institute of the Motor Industry.
G.Inst.M.	Graduate of the Institute of Marketing.
G.Inst.P.	Graduate of the Institute of Physics.
G.M.	George Medal.
G.M.A.S.I.	Graduate Member of the Ambulance Service Institute.
G.Mus.R.N.C.M.	Graduate in Music of the Royal Northern College of Music.
G.N.S.M.	Graduate of the Northern School of Music.
Grad.B.H.I.	Graduate of the British Horological Institute.
Grad.I.A.P.	Graduate of the Institution of Analysts and Programmers.

191

Grad.I.Elecl.E.	Graduate of the Institution of Electrical and Electronics Incorporated Engineers.
Grad.I.I.Sec.	Graduate of the Institute of Industrial Security.
Grad.I.M.A.	Graduate Member of the Institute of Mathematics and its Applications.
Grad.I.Manf.	Graduate Member of the Institute of Manufacturing.
Grad.I.M.F.	Graduate of the Institute of Metal Finishing.
Grad.I.M.S.	Graduate of the Institute of Management Specialists.
Grad.Inst.B.E.	Graduate Member of the Institute of British Engineers.
Grad.Inst.B.T.M.	Graduate of the Institute of Business and Technical Management.
Grad.Inst.N.D.T.	Graduate of the British Institute of Non-Destructive Testing.
Grad.Inst.P.S.	Graduate of the Institute of Purchasing and Supply.
Grad.I.O.P.	Graduate of the Institute of Printing.
Grad.I.P.M.	Graduate of the Institute of Personnel Management.
Grad.I.S.	Graduate Member of the Institute of Statisticians.
Grad.I.S.M.	Graduate of the Institute of Supervisory Management.
Grad.N.I.H.	Graduate of the National Institute of Hardware.
Grad.P.R.I.	Graduate of the Plastics and Rubber Institute.
Grad.R.S.C.	Graduate of the Royal Society of Chemistry.
Grad.S.C.P.	Graduate of the Society of Certified Professionals.
Grad.S.L.A.E.T.	Graduate of the Society of Licensed Aircraft Engineers and Technologists.
Grad.I.Elec.I.E.	Graduate of the Institution of Electrical and Electronics Incorporated Engineers.

Grad.Weld.I.	Graduate of the Welding Institute.
G.R.I.C.	Graduate Membership of the Royal Institute of Chemistry.
G.R.N.C.M.	Graduate of the Royal Northern College of Music.
G.R.S.C.	Graduate of the Royal Society of Chemistry.
G.R.S.M.	Graduate Diploma of the Royal Manchester School of Music.
G.R.S.M.(Hons)	Graduate of the Royal Schools of Music.
G.T.C.L.	Graduate Diploma of Trinity College of Music, London.
H.Chir.D.	Diploma in Higher Chiropodial Theory of the Institute of Chiropodists.
H.N.C.	Higher National Certificate.
H.N.D.	Higher National Diploma.
Hon.F.C.P.	Charter Fellow of the College of Preceptors.
H.V.Cert.	Health Visitors Certificate.
I.P.F.A.	Member of the Chartered Institute of Public Finance and Accountancy.
J.P.	Justice of the Peace.
K.B.E.	Knight Commander of the Order of the British Empire.
K.C.B.	Knight Commander of the Bath.
K.C.H.	Knight Commander of Hanover.
K.C.M.G.	Knight Commander of St. Michael and St. George.
K.C.V.O.	Knight Commander of the Royal Victorian Order.
K.G.	Knight of the Order of the Garter.
K.M.	Knight of Malta.
K.T.	Knight of the Order of the Thistle.

APPENDIX B

L.A.A.I.	Licentiate of the Institute of Administrative Accountants.
L.A.B.A.C.	Licentiate Member of the Association of Business and Administrative Computing.
L.A.M.R.T.P.I.	Legal Associate Member of the Royal Town Planning Institute.
L.A.S.I.	Licentiate of the Ambulance Service Institute.
L.B.E.I.	Licentiate of the Institution of Body Engineers.
L.B.I.P.P.	Licentiate of the British Institute of Professional Photography.
L.B.I.S.T.	Licentiate of the British Institute of Surgical Technologists.
L.B.S.C.	Licentiate of the British Society of Commerce.
L.C.E.A.	Licentiate of the Association of Cost and Executive Accountants.
L.Ch.	Licentiate in Chiropody of the Institute of Chiropodists.
L.C.P.	Licentiate of the College of Preceptors.
L.C.S.I.	Licentiate of the Construction Surveyors' Institute.
L.C.S.P.(B.Th.)	London and Counties School of Physiology – Diploma in Health and Beauty Therapy.
LC.S.T.	Licentiate of the College of Speech Therapists.
L.D.S.	Licentiate in Dental Surgery.
L.D.S.R.C.P.S.Glas.	Licentiate in Dental Surgery of the Royal College of Physicians and Surgeons of Glasgow.
L.D.S.R.C.S.Ed.	Licentiate in Dental Surgery of the Royal College of Surgeons of Edinburgh.
L.D.S.R.C.S.Eng.	Licentiate in Dental Surgery of the Royal College of Surgeons of England.
L.F.B.A.	Licentiate of the Corporation of Executives and Administrators.

194

L.F.C.I.	Licentiate of the Faculty of Commerce and Industry.
L.F.C.S.	Licentiate of the Faculty of Secretaries.
L.F.S.	Licentiate of the Faculty of Architects and Surveyors (Surveyors)
L.G.C.L.	Licentiate of the Guild of Cleaners and Launderers.
L.G.S.M.	Licentiate of the Guildhall School of Music and Drama.
L.H.A.	Licentiate of the Institute of Health Service Administrators.
L.H.C.I.M.A.	Licentiate of the Hotel, Catering and Institutional Management Association.
L.H.G.	Licentiate of the Institute of Heraldic and Genealogical Studies.
L.Ac.	Licentiate of Acupuncture.
L.I.C.W.	Licentiate of the Institute of Clerks of Works.
L.I.L.A.M.	Licentiate of the Institute of Leisure and Amenity Management.
L.I.M.	Licentiate of the Institute of Metals.
L.I.M.A.	Licentiate of the Institute of Mathematics and its Applications.
L.I.M.F.	Licentiate of the Institute of Metal Finishing.
L.Inst.B.B.	Licentiate of the Institute of British Bakers.
L.Inst.B.C.A.	Licentiate of the Institute of Burial and Cremation Administration.
L.I.R.	Licentiate of the Institute of Population Registration.
L.I.S.T.D.	Licentiate of the Imperial Society of Teachers of Dancing.
Litt.D.	Doctors of Letters.
Ll.B.	Bachelor of Law.
L.L.C.M.	Licentiate of the London College of Music.
Ll.D.	Doctor of Laws
Ll.M.	Master of Laws.

L.L.M.R.C.P.(Ire.) L.L.M.R.C.S.(Ire.)	Conjoint Diplomas of Licentiate and Licentiate in Midwifery of the Royal College of Physicians and Surgeons of Ireland.
L.L.S.P.T.	Licentiate of the London School of Polymer Technology.
L.M.P.A.	Qualified Member of the Master Photographers Association.
L.M.R.T.P.I.	Legal Member of the Royal Town Planning Institute.
L.M.S.S.A.Lon.	Licentiate in Medicine, Surgery and Midwidery of the Society of Apothecaries of London.
L.Mus.L.C.M.	Licentiate in Music of the London College of Music.
L.Mus.T.C.L.	Licentiate in Music of Trinity College of Music, London.
L.P.R.I.	Licentiate of the Plastics and Rubber Institute.
L.R.A.D.	Licentiate of the Royal Academy of Dancing.
L.R.A.M.	Licentiate of Royal Academy of Music.
L.R.C.P.Edin. L.R.C.S.Edin. L.R.C.P.S.Glas.	Conjoint Diplomas of Licentiate of the Royal College of Physicians of Edinburgh, Royal College of Surgeons of Edinburgh, Royal College of Physicians and Surgeons of Glasgow.
L.R.P.S.	Licentiate of the Royal Photographic Society.
L.R.S.C.	Licentiate of the Royal Society of Chemistry.
L.R.S.M.	Licentiate of the Royal Schools of Music.
L.S.C.P.(Assoc.)	Associate of the London and Counties Society of Physiologists.
L.T.C.L.	Licentiate of Trinity College of Music, London.
L.Th.	Licentiate in Theology.
L.V.O.	Lieutenant of the Royal Victorian Order.

M.A.	Master of Arts.
M.A.(Arch.St.)	Master of Arts (Architectural Studies).
M.A.B.A.C.	Member of the Association of Business and Administrative Computing.
M.A.B.E.	Member of the Association of Business Executives.
M.Ac.A.	Master of the Acupuncture Association and Register.
M.Acc.	Master of Accountancy.
M.A.C.E.	Member of the Association of Conference Executives.
M.A.C.P.	Member of the Assocation of Computer Professionals.
M.A.(Econ.)	Master of Arts in Economic and Social Studies.
M.A.(Ed.)	Master of Arts in Education.
M.Agr.	Master of Agriculture.
M.Agr.Sc.	Master of Agricultural Science.
M.A.I.E.	Member of the British Association of Industrial Editors.
M.A.(L.D.)	Master of Arts (Landscape Design).
M.A.M.S.	Member of the Association of Medical Secretaries, Practice Administrators and Receptionists.
M.A.(Mus.)	Master of Arts (Music).
M.Anim.Sc.	Master of Animal Science.
M.A.O.	Master of Obstetrics.
M.App.Sci.	Master of Applied Science.
M.A.P.S.A.S.	Member of the Association of Public Service Administrative Staff.
M.Ar.Ad.	Master of Archive Administration.
M.A.(R.C.A.)	Master of Arts, Royal College of Art.
M.Arch.	Master of Architecture.
M.A.S.E.E.	Member of the Association of Supervisory and Executive Engineers.
M.A.(Soc.Sci.)	Master of Arts (Social Science).

197

M.A.(Theol.)	Master of Arts in Theology.
M.B.A.	Master of Business Administration.
M.B.A.E.	Member of the British Association of Electrolysis.
M.B.,B.Ch.	Conjoint degree of Batchelor of Medicine, Bachelor of Surgery.
M.B.,B.Chir.	Conjoint degree of Bachelor of Medicine, Bachelor of Surgery, University of Cambridge.
M.B.,B.S.	Conjoint degree of Bachelor of Medicine, Bachelor of Surgery, University of London and University of Newcastle.
M.B.,Ch.B.	Conjoint degree of Bachelor of Medicine, Bachelor of Surgery.
M.B.C.O.	Member of the British College of Ophthalmic Opticians.
M.B.C.S.	Member of the British Computer Society.
M.B.E.	Member of the Order of the British Empire.
M.B.E.I.	Member of the Institute of Body Engineers.
M.B.E.S.	Member of the Bureau of Engineer Surveyors.
M.B.H.A.	Member of the British Hypnotherapy Association.
M.B.H.I.	Member of the British Horological Institute.
M.B.I.D.	Member of the British Institute of Interior Design.
M.B.I.E.	Member of the British Institute of Embalmers.
M.B.I.I.	Member of the British Institute of Innkeeping.
M.B.I.M.	Member of the British Institute of Management.
M.B.Sc.	Master in Business Science.
M.C.A.A.	Member of the Faculty of Community Accountancy and Administration.
M.C.A.M.	Member of the Communication Advertising and Marketing Education Foundation.

M.C.B.	Mastership in Clinical Biochemistry.
M.C.D.	Master of Civic Design.
M.C.D.H.	Master of Community Dental Health.
M.C.F.I.	Member of the Clothing and Footwear Institute.
M.Ch.	Master of Surgery.
M.Ch.D.	Master of Dental Surgery.
M.Chir.	Master of Surgery.
M.Ch.Orth.	Master of Orthopaedic Surgery.
M.Ch.S.	Member of the Society of Chiropodists.
M.C.I.	Member of the Institute of Commerce.
M.C.I.B.S.	Member of the Chartered Institution of Building Services.
M.C.I.O.B.	Member of the Chartered Institute of Building.
M.C.I.T.	Member of the Chartered Institute of Transport.
M.Coll.P.	Member of the College of Preceptors.
M.Comm.	Master of Commerce.
M.Comm.H.	Master of Community Health.
M.C.P.M.	Member of the Confederation of Professional Management.
M.C.S.I.	Member of the Construction Surveyors' Institute.
M.C.S.P.	Member of the Chartered Society of Physiotherapy.
M.C.T.	Member of the Association of Corporate Treasurers.
M.C.	Military Cross.
M.D.	Doctor of Medicine.
M.D.C.R.	Management Diploma of the College of Radiographers.
M.Des.	Master of Design.
M.Des.(R.C.A.)	Master of Design, Royal College of Art.
M.D.S.	Master of Dental Surgery.

199

M.D.Sc.	Master of Dental Science.
M.E.C.I.	Member of the Institute of Employment Consultants.
M.Ed.	Master of Education.
M.Ed.(Ed.Psych)	Master of Education (Educational Psychology).
M.Ed.Stud.	Master of Educational Studies.
M.Eng.	Master of Engineering.
M.F.A.	Master of Fine Art.
M.F.C.	Mastership in Food Control.
M.F.C.M.	Member of the Faculty of Community Medicine.
M.F.D.O.	Member of the Faculty of Dispensing Opticians.
M.F.T.Com.	Member of the Faculty of Teachers in Commerce.
M.G.D.S.R.C.S.Ed.	Membership in General Dental Surgery, Royal College of Surgeons of Edinburgh.
M.G.D.S.R.C.S.Eng.	Membership in General Dental Surgery, Royal College of Surgeons of England.
M.H.C.I.M.A.	Member of the Hotel, Catering and Institutional Management Association.
M.Hort.(R.H.S.)	National Diploma in Horticulture, Royal Horticultural Society.
M.H.T.T.A.	Member of the Highway and Traffic Technicians Association.
M.I.A.A.	Member of the Incorporated Association of Architects and Surveyors (Architects).
M.I.A.E.A.	Member of the Institute of Automotive Engineer Assessors.
M.I.Agr.E.	Member of the Institution of Agricultural Engineers.
M.I.A.P.	Member of the Institution of Analysts and Programmers.
M.I.A.S.	Member of the Incorporated Association of Architects and Surveyors (Surveyors).

M.I.A.T.	Member of the Institute of Asphalt Technology.
M.I.B.C.O.	Member of the Institution of Building Control Officers.
M.I.B.F.	Member of the Institute of British Foundrymen.
M.I.Biol.	Member of the Institute of Biology.
M.I.C.D.	Member of the Institute of Creative Design.
M.I.C.E.	Member of the Institution of Civil Engineers.
M.I.Chem.E.	Member of the Institution of Chemical Engineers.
M.I.C.M.	Associate Member of the Institute of Credit Management.
M.I.C.O.	Member of the Institute of Careers Officers.
M.I.Corr.S.T.	Member of the Institution of Corrosion Science and Technology.
M.I.C.S.	Member of the Institute of Chartered Shipbrokers.
M.I.C.W.	Member of the Institute of Clerks of Works.
M.I.D.T.A.	Member of the International Dance Teachers' Association.
M.I.E.D.	Member of the Institution of Engineering Designers.
M.I.E.E.	Member of the Institution of Electrical Engineers.
M.I.Elect.I.E.	Corporate Member of the Institution of Electrical and Electronics Incorporated Engineers.
M.I.E.M.	Master Member of the Institute of Executives and Managers.
M.I.E.R.E.	Member of the Institution of Electronic and Radio Engineers.
M.I.Ex.	Member of the Institute of Export.
M.I.Ex.E.	Member of the Institute of Executive Engineers and Officers.

APPENDIX B

M.I.Exp.E.	Member of the Institute of Explosives Engineers.
M.I.Fire E.	Member of the Institution of Fire Engineers.
M.I.Gas E.	Member of the Institution of Gas Engineers.
M.I.G.D.	Member of the Institute of Grocery Distribution.
M.I.Geol.	Member of the Institute of Geologists.
M.I.H.	Member of the Institute of Housing.
M.I.H.Ec.	Member of the Institute of Home Economics.
M.I.H.E.	Member of the Institution of Highway Engineers.
M.I.H.T.C.M.	Member of the Institute of Hotel, Tourism and Catering Management.
M.I.I.M.	Member of the Institution of Industrial Managers.
M.I.Inf.Sc.	Member of the Institute of Information Scientists.
M.I.I.R.S.M.	Member of the International Institute of Risk and Safety Management.
M.I.I.S.E.	Member of the International Institute of Social Economics.
M.I.I.Sec.	Member of the Institute of Industrial Security.
M.I.L.	Member of the Institute of Linguists.
M.I.L.A.M.	Member of the Institute of Leisure and Amenity Management.
M.I.M.	Member of the Institute of Metals.
M.I.Manf.	Member of the Institute of Manufacturing.
M.I.Mar.E.	Member of the Institute of Marine Engineers.
M.I.M.B.M.	Member of the Institute of Municipal Building Management.
M.I.M.C.	Member of th Institute of Management Consultants.
M.I.Mech.E.	Member of the Institution of Mechanical Engineers.

202

M.I.M.F.	Member of the Institute of Metal Finishing.
M.I.M.G.Tech.E.	Member of the Institution of Mechanical Engineers and General Technician Engineers.
M.I.M.H.	Member of the Institute of Materials Handling.
M.I.M.I.	Member of the Institute of the Motor Industry.
M.I.Min.E.	Member of the Institution of Mining Engineers.
M.I.M.I.T.	Member of the Institute of Musical Instrument Technology.
M.I.M.M.	Member of the Institute of Male Masseurs.
M.I.M.M.	Member of the Institution of Mining and Metallurgy.
M.I.M.S.	Member of the Institute of Management Specialists.
M.Inst.A.E.A.	Member of the Institute of Automotive Engineer Assessors.
M.Inst.A.M.	Member of the Institute of Administrative Management.
M.Inst.B.B.	Member of the Institute of British Bakers.
M.Inst.B.C.A.	Member of the Institute of Burial and Cremation Administration.
M.Inst.B.E.	Member of the Institute of British Engineers.
M.Inst.B.R.M.	Member of the Institute of Baths and Recreation Management.
M.Inst.B.T.M.	Member of the Institute of Business and Technical Management.
M.Inst.C.F.	Member of the Institute of Carpet Fitters.
M.Inst.C.M.	Member of the Institute of Commercial Management.
M.Inst.E.	Member of the Institute of Energy.
M.Inst.F.F.	Member of the Institute of Freight Forwarders.
M.Inst.M.	Member of the Institute of Marketing.

M.Inst.M.C.	Member of the Institute of Measurement and Control.
M.Inst.M.E.	Member of the International Institute of Management Executives.
M.Inst.N.D.T.	Member of the British Institute of Non-Destructive Testing.
M.Inst.P.	Member of the Institute of Physics.
M.Inst.Pet.	Member of the Institute of Petroleum.
M.inst.Pkg.	Member of the Institute of Packaging.
M.Inst.P.M.	Full Member of the Institute of Professional Managers.
M.Inst.P.S.	Corporate Member of the Institute of Purchasing and Supply.
M.Inst.R.	Member of the Institute of Refrigeration.
M.Inst.S.M.M.	Member of the Institute of Sales and Marketing Management.
M.Inst.T.A.	Member of the Institute of Transport Administration.
M.Inst.W.M.	Member of the Institute of Wastes Management.
M.I.O.P.	Member of the Institute of Printing.
M.I.P.	Member of the Institute of Plumbing.
M.I.P.A.	Member of the Institute of Practitioners in Advertising.
M.I.P.C.	Member of the Institute of Production Control.
M.I.P.H.E.	Member of the Institute of Public Health Engineers.
M.I.P.I.	Member of the Institute of Professional Investigators.
M.I.Plant E.	Member of the Institution of Plant Engineers.
M.I.P.M.	Member of the Institute of Personnel Management.
M.I.P.R.	Member of the Institute of Public Relations.
M.I.Q.	Member of the Institute of Quarrying.

M.I.Q.A.	Member of the Institute of Quality Assurance.
M.I.R.	Member of the Institute of Population Registration.
M.I.R.S.E.	Member of the Institution of Railway Signal Engineers.
M.I.R.T.	Member of the Institute of Reprographic Technology.
M.I.R.T.E.	Member of the Institute of Road Transport Engineering.
M.I.S.	Member of the Institute of Statisticians.
M.I.S.M.	Member of the Institute of Supervisory Management.
M.I.S.O.B.	Member of the Incorporated Society of Organ Builders.
M.I.S.T.	Member of the Institute of Science Technology
M.I.S.T.C.	Member of the Institute of Scientific and Technical Communicators.
M.I.S.T.C.	Member of ths International Sports Therapy Council.
M.I.S.T.M.	Member of the Institute of Sales Technology and Management.
M.I.Struct.E.	Member of the Institution of Structural Engineers.
M.I.S.W.	Member of the Institute of Social Welfare.
M.I.T.D.	Member of the Institute of Training and Development.
M.I.T.S.A.	Member of the Institute of Trading Standards Administration.
M.I.W.H.T.E.	Member of the Instiution of Works and Highways Technician Engineers.
M.I.W.P.C.	Member of the Institute of Water Pollution Control.
M.Jur.	Master of Jurisprudence.
M.L.C.O.M.	Member of the London College of Osteopathic Medicine.

M.L.D.	Master of Landscape Design.
M.Ling.	Master of Languages.
M.Litt.	Master of Letters.
M.L.S.	Master of Library Science.
M.M.	Military Medal.
M.M.A.	Master of Management and Administration.
M.Med.Sci.	Master of Medical Science.
M.Met.	Master of Metallurgy.
M.M.S.	Member of the Institute of Management Services.
M.M.Sc.	Master of Medical Sciences.
M.Mus.	Master of Music.
M.Mus.R.C.M.	Degree of Master of Music, Royal College of Music.
M.N.	Master of Nursing.
M.N.A.E.A.	Member of the National Association of Estate Agents.
M.N.I.	Member of the Nautical Institute.
M.N.I.H.	Member of the National Institute of Hardware.
M.N.I.M.H.	Member of the National Institute of Medical Herbalists.
M.Obst.G.	Master of Obstetrics and Gynaecology.
M.P.A.	Master of Public Administration.
M.P.H.	Master of Public Health.
M.Pharm.	Master of Pharmacy.
M.Phil.	Master of Philosophy.
M.Phil.(Eng.)	Master of Philosophy in Engineering.
M.P.P.S.	Master of Public Policy Studies.
M.P.R.I.	Member of the Plastics and Rubber Institute.
M.P.S.	Member of the Pharmaceutical Society.
M.Psych.Med.	Master of Psychological Medicine.
M.Psychol.	Master of Psychology.
M.Rad.	Master of Radiology.

M.R.Ae.S.	Member of the Royal Aeronautical Society.
M.R.C.G.P.	Member of the Royal College of General Practitioners.
M.R.C.O.G.	Member of the Royal College of Obstetricians and Gynaecologists.
M.R.C.P.	Member of the Royal College of Physicians.
M.R.C.Path.	Member of the Royal College of Pathologists.
M.R.C.Psych.	Member of the Royal College of Psychiatrists.
M.R.C.R.	Member of the Royal College of Radiologists.
M.R.C.S.Eng.	Member of the Royal College of Surgeons of England.
M.R.C.V.S.	Member of the Royal College of Veterinary Surgeons.
M.R.E.H.I.S.	Member of the Royal Environmental Health Institute of Scotland.
M.R.I.N.	Member of the Royal Institute of Navigation.
M.R.I.N.A.	Member of the Royal Institution of Naval Architects.
M.R.I.P.H.H.	Member of the Royal Institute of Public Health and Hygiene.
M.R.O.	Member of the Register of Osteopaths.
M.R.S.C.	Member of the Royal Society of Chemistry.
M.R.S.H.	Member of the Royal Society of Health.
M.R.T.P.I.	Member of the Royal Town Planning Institute.
M.S.M.	Meritorious Service Medal.
M.S.	Master of Surgery.
M.S.B.P.	Associate of the Society of Business Practitioners.
M.S.B.Th.	Member of the Society of Health and Beauty Therapists.
M.Sc.	Master of Science.

APPENDIX B

M.Sc.D.	Master of Dental Science.
M.Sc.Econ.	Master of Faculty of Economic and Social Studies.
M.Sc.(Econ.)	Master of Science in Economics.
M.Sc.(Ed.)	Master of Science in Education.
M.Sc.(Eng.)	Master of Science in Engineering.
M.Sc.(Mgt.)	Master of Science in Management.
M.S.C.P.	Member of the Society of Certified Professionals.
M.S.C.T.	Member of the Society of Cardiological Technicians.
M.Sc.Tech.	Master of Technical Science.
M.S.E.	Member of the Society of Engineers.
M.S.E.R.T.	Member of the Society of Electronic and Radio Technicians.
M.S.H.A.A.	Member of the Society of Hearing Aid Audiologists.
M.S.I.A.D.	Member of ths Society of Industrial Artists and Designers.
M.S.L.A.E.T.	Member of the Society of Licensed Aircraft Engineers and Technologists.
M.Soc.Sc.	Master of Social Science.
M.S.R.G.R.	Member of the Society of Remedial Gymnasts.
M.S.Sc.	Master of Surgical Science.
M.S.S.T.	Member of the Society of Surveying Technicians.
M.St.	Master of Studies.
M.S.T.A.	Member of the Swimming Teachers' Association.
M.S.W.	Master in Social Work.
M.T.D.	Master of Transport Design.
M.Tech.	Master of Technology.
M.Th.	Master of Theology.
M.T.P.	Master of Town and Country Planning.

M.Trop.Med.	Master of Tropical Medicine.
M.Univ.	Master of the University (honorary).
Mus.B.	Bachelor of Music.
Mus.D.	Doctor of Music.
Mus.M.	Master of Music.
Mus.M.(Comp.)	Master of Music (Composition).
Mus.M.(Perf.)	Master of Music (Performance.)
M.V.M.	Master of Veterinary Medicine.
M.V.Sc.	Master of Veterinary Science.
M.Weld.I.	Member of the Welding Institute.
M.W.E.S.	Member of the Women's Engineering Society.
N.C.A.	National Certificate in Agriculture.
N.D.	Diploma in Naturopathy.
N.D.D.	National Diploma in Design.
N.D.H.	National Diploma in Horticulture.
N.D.S.F.	National Diploma of the Society of Floristry.
N.D.T.	National Diploma in the Science and Practice of Turfculture and Sports Ground Management.
N.N.E.B.	National Nursery Examination Board.
O.B.E.	Officer of the Order of the British Empire.
O.M.	Order of Merit.
O.N.C.	Ordinary National Certificate.
O.N.D.	Ordinary National Diploma.
P.C.	Privy Counsellor.
P.E.S.D.	Private and Executive Secretary's Diploma.
Ph.D.	Doctor of Philosophy.
P.M.R.A.F.N.S.	Princess Mary's Royal Air Force Nursing Service.

P.P.L.	Private Pilot's Licence.
P.S.C.	Private Secretary's Certificate.
Q.A.R.A.N.C.	Queen Alexandra's Royal Army Nursing Corps.
Q.A.R.N.N.S.	Queeen Alexandra's Royal Naval Nursing Service.
Q.C.	Queen's Counsel.
Q.F.S.M.	Queen's Fire Service Medal.
Q.P.M.	Queen's Police Medal.
R.A.	Royal Academician.
R.A.F.	Royal Air Force.
R.G.N.	Registered General Nurse.
R.J.Dip.	Diploma for Retail Jewellers.
R.M.	Registered Midwife.
R.M.Inst.C.F.	Registered Member of the Institute of Carpet Fitters.
R.M.N.	Registered Mental Nurse.
R.N.	Royal Navy.
R.N.M.H.	Registered Nurse for the Mentally Handicapped.
R.P.	Registered Plumber.
R.S.C.N.	Registered Sick Children's Nurse.
S.G.M.	Sea Gallantry Medal.
Sc.D.	Doctor of Science.
S.C.P.L.	Senior Commercial Pilot's Licence.
S.Eng.F.Inst.S.M.M.	Qualified Sales Engineer of the Institute of Sales and Marketing Management.
S.L.C.	Secretarial Language Certificate.
S.L.D.	Secretarial Language Diploma.
S.R.D.	State Registered Dietician.
S.R.N.	State Registered Nurse.
S.S.C.	Secretarial Studies Certificate.

T.Cert.	Teacher's Certificate.
T.D.	Territorial Decoration.
V.A.D.	Voluntary Aid Detachment.
V.C.	Victoria Cross.
V.D.	Volunteer Officers Decoration.
W.R.V.S.	Women's Royal Voluntary Service.

Appendix C

THE WIDELY RECOGNISED DAYS FOR
FLYING THE UNION FLAG

February 6th	Her Majesty's Accession.
February 19th	Birthday of The Duke of York.
March 1st	St. David's Day.
March 10th	Birthday of The Prince Edward.
March*	Commonwealth Day.
April 21st	Birthday of Her Majesty The Queen.
April 23rd	St. George's Day.
June 2nd	Coronation Day.
June 10th	Birthday of The Duke of Edinburgh.
On a date appointed in June	Queen's Official Birthday.
July 1st	Birthday of The Princess of Wales.
August 4th	Birthday of Her Majesty Queen Elizabeth the Queen Mother.
August 15th	Birthday of The Princess Anne.
August 21st	Birthday of The Princess Margaret.
November†	Remembrance Sunday.

* Commonwealth Day is the second Monday in March.
† Remembrance Sunday is the second Sunday in November.

November 14th	Birthday of The Prince of Wales.
November 20th	Her Majesty's Wedding Day.
November 30th	St. Andrew's Day.

Other occasions by special command of Her Majesty and notified in the press by the Department of the Environment.

Appendix D
A LIST OF BOOKS WHICH WILL BE FOUND USEFUL

A Chambers or Concise Oxford Dictionary.

Whitaker's Almanack.

Roget's Thesaurus of English Words and Phrases.
  (There is now a Penguin Reference Books Edition of this work.)

Pear's Cyclopaedia.

Stevenson's Book of Quotations, or a less expensive publication—
  Everyman's Dictionary of Quotations and Proverbs by D.C. Browning.

Debrett's Correct Form.

The Complete Plain Words by Sir Ernest Gowers, published by H.M.S.O.

Who's Who.

Titles and Forms of Address, published by A. & C. Black.

The Municipal Year Book.

Civic Ceremonial by G. N. Waldram, M.V.O., published by Shaw and Sons.

The Councillor by John Prophet, M.A. published by Shaw and Sons.

Simple Heraldry Cheerfully Illustrated by Moncrieffe and Pottinger, published by Nelson.

Ribbons and Medals by Captain H. Taprell Dorling, D.S.O., R.N. (Taffrail) in association with L. F. Guille, published by George Philip and Son Ltd.

An A.B.C. of Chairmanship by Walter Citrine.

The Manor and the Borough, by the late Sidney and Beatrice Webb.

The following more costly publications are available in Reference Libraries—

Bartlett's Familiar Quotations.

Burke's Peerage.

Debrett.

Encyclopedia Britannica.

Kelly's handbook.

Boutell's Heraldry.

Boutell's Heraldry. Revised by J. P. Brooke-Little, 1983. Published by Frederick Warne (Publishers) Ltd., London.

Civic and Corporate Heraldry—A dictionary of Impersonal Arms of England, Wales and Northern Ireland. Compiled and edited by Geoffrey Briggs, F.R.S.A., F.S.A.(Scot.). Published by Heraldry Today, 10 Beauchamp Place, London S.W.1.

216

INDEX

217

INDEX

INDEX